FOUNDER TO FOUNDER

Tips and tales from
100 entrepreneurs and investors

KATE KIRK
with
PETER and **ALAN COWLEY**

Published by Invested Investor Limited
This is edition one, in 2019

www.investedinvestor.com

Text and cover designed by Paul Parrett Book Production, www.pbbp.co.uk
Illustrations by Neil Kerber

ISBN
978-1-9164079-5-4 (paperback)
978-1-9164079-1-6 (ebook)

Contents

About the authors

Kate Kirk has been writing about technology, entrepreneurship and management for over a decade. She has written two books on the technology cluster known as 'the Cambridge Phenomenon', has covered the history of technology transfer at the University of Cambridge, and worked with Peter on his first book, *The Invested Investor*. She is a regular speaker on all aspects of entrepreneurship in the Cambridge technology ecosystem and continues to research the history and development of the cluster.

Peter Cowley is a serial entrepreneur and angel investor. He was brought up in Hull and has kept his Yorkshire honesty. He has founded and run a dozen businesses and has invested his own money in more than 70 start-ups. He is the President of the European Business Angel Network and was UK Angel of the Year 2014. He has mentored hundreds of entrepreneurs and is currently on the board of eight start-ups. Peter founded and runs Martlet, the investment arm of the Marshall of Cambridge Group, a privately owned 100-year-old engineering company. He is the former chair of the Cambridge Angels and is a Fellow in Entrepreneurship at the University of Cambridge Judge Business School. He was a non-executive director of the UK Business Angel Association and on the investment committee of the UK Angel CoFund. He is a popular speaker and travels the world sharing his experiences, good and bad, with entrepreneurs and angel investors.

Alan Cowley co-founded The Invested Investor with his father, Peter, in 2017. The mission of The Invested Investor is to improve the business creation journey for entrepreneurs and investors by helping them to understand each other better and work together more transparently and productively. It does this through sharing lessons and stories from people working in all aspects of the start-up ecosystem, which are available as podcasts via the website www.investedinvestor.com. The Invested Investor book distils these lessons for angels and would-be angels, and was published in 2018. Alan is also a Director of Camdata Ltd.

Acknowledgements

We're extremely grateful to the many entrepreneurs and investors who gave up their time to be interviewed for the Invested Investor podcast series or who answered our survey about the challenges they face. Their real-life stories have given us a huge range of insights into the start-up world and this book wouldn't have been possible without them. Too numerous to list here, their names and brief biographical details are included in the last section of the book.

We're also very grateful to Soraya Jones, Wendy Smalley, Brian Harris and Ludo Chapman, who have contributed to this project in numerous ways and offered extremely helpful ideas and advice.

CHAPTER 1

Introduction

6 Ideas are one thing. Putting them into action is completely different.

The Invested Investor team are on a mission to improve the journeys of start-ups by educating investors and entrepreneurs, so that – hopefully – they understand each other better, make fewer mistakes and have a better chance of success.

The statistics on survival rates for new businesses are stark. The US Bureau of Labor Statistics estimated, based on 2017 figures, that 20% of start-ups fail in their first year, and by year five, 50% have failed. By year ten, only 30% are still operating. In the UK, the Office for National Statistics has the five-year failure rate at 60%; the equivalent body in Australia asserts that the failure rate there is faster, with 60% of new businesses disappearing within three years.

So, it's hard out there in the start-up world, and anything you can do to make the journey easier as a would-be entrepreneur should be welcomed. One of the best ways to learn is to hear from others who have been in similar positions and to try and avoid the mistakes they made, or to identify what they did to be successful and how it might translate into your business.

Since 2017, the Invested Investor team has interviewed around 120 investors and entrepreneurs to find out what makes them tick and the challenges they have faced. The website www.investedin-vestor.com features almost 100 podcasts and articles based on the interviews. Our first book, *The Invested Investor*, compiled some of these war stories into a step-by-step journey from how investors get started to the things they need to do to invest as wisely and as safely as possible, and what to expect at exit. We looked closely at what it takes to be an angel investor, so that readers who were trying to decide whether or not to begin investing in start-ups had the information they needed to make the right choice for themselves.

Now it's time to do the same thing for entrepreneurs. Many of the investors we interviewed started out as entrepreneurs, so we've gone back to their stories to draw out the lessons they learned along that part of their journey. We've also interviewed numerous entrepreneurs, many of whom are still in the start-up phase, while others have seen successful and less-successful exits and are still going back for more. A number of founders and CEOs of early-stage companies also responded to our survey about the three biggest challenges they've faced so far, which showed us what start-ups find most difficult as they get off the ground and start to grow. All of our interviewees and contributors are quoted throughout the book, and many of them have had multiple roles as entrepreneurs, investors and advisers. Rather than repeat their details every time we hear from them, we've listed them alphabetically at the back of the book, along with a brief description of their role(s) at the time of writing.

There are clearly common challenges for all fledgling businesses – coming up with a viable business plan, getting funding, building the team, finding customers, and so on – but there are always subtle and not-so-subtle differences. Hearing from many voices across many different sectors, as you will in this book, helps to illuminate the kinds of issues you're going to face, and the way different entrepreneurs have solved them. As one of our interviewees said, 'It's really important to listen to advice. If you can avoid making the same mistakes as other people, why wouldn't you?'

> My number one tip to any entrepreneur starting out in business today would be to hire good people, make something that other people care about, and spend as little money as possible doing it. If you do those three things, essentially you'll have a team that builds a product that somebody is interested in, and you'll get to a point, hopefully, of product–market fit before you run out of cash. From then on, there is a host of other challenges to solve.
>
> Luke Hakes, investor

In this book, we'll look at what life is like as an entrepreneur, whether you should start your company with a co-founder, how to build your core team in the early days – when each hire is critical – and the relationships with investors, the board and any advisors and mentors you collect along the way. We'll also see how various entrepreneurs have found their customers or created a market, how they've made decisions about intellectual property, and what they've learned about cash flow. We look at scaling and pivoting, when companies suddenly find themselves carrying out functions they never anticipated or entering markets that weren't mentioned in the business plan. Given the statistics on business failures that we've quoted above, there are, of course, stories without happy endings, but there are also stories of successful exits to show you the upside.

But first, why do you want to become an entrepreneur? You might have picked up this book because you're simply curious, or because you've always wanted to start your own business, or because you have an abiding passion that you can no longer resist.

People start businesses for all sorts of reasons, and sometimes they even start businesses by accident, as we will find out. So your first test is to think about why you want to be an entrepreneur and what it will mean to you.

Some of our interviewees seem to have tried quite hard to put people off becoming an entrepreneur at all. We're told that people who follow their passion never do a day's work in their lives – because work doesn't feel like work at all. But is that really true? Our interviewees point out that following your passion can mean putting in 20-hour days and collapsing exhausted for a few hours' sleep before doing it all over again. Following your passion can mean giving up things you take for granted – your car, your flat, your social life, holidays. Following your passion can mean constantly being told you'll never make it, and having to pick yourself up from failure again and again. Not such a rosy picture, is it?

> Don't do it. Save your marriage. Save your assets. You don't need it…The badge of a start-up is chronic fatigue syndrome. The badge of a start-up is grey hairs on the side of your head. The badge of a start-up is your shaky relationship with your better half. Those are the things that come with trying to build a start-up.
>
> Dominic Hill, entrepreneur

Of course, it isn't all bad – otherwise no-one would want to be an entrepreneur. There are plenty of examples of successful entrepreneurs who have come through the hard times and have become household names. And there are plenty of other successful entrepreneurs who avoid the limelight and simply get on with building their businesses. Could you be one of them? Could you get to the point where 20-hour days don't feel like work?

> It doesn't really feel like a job, because we love what we do. We have purpose in what we're doing. It will be tumultuous, it will be rocky, but if you can take that type of pressure, and if you can enjoy it, and if the endgame is a dream of yours,

something that gives you goose bumps and you can't live without, then you're on the right path.

Priya Lakhani, entrepreneur

But don't worry if you don't have that overriding passion, you might still find that you're an entrepreneur underneath; you just need a nudge. Some entrepreneurs never set out to start a business. They simply find themselves in a situation where founding a company sounds like a good idea, or is the right thing to do. In the case of Hermann Hauser, co-founder of Acorn Computers in the 1970s and subsequently a noted serial entrepreneur and investor, the first step was actually determined by the price of setting up a company in the UK.

Chris Curry came to see me and said, "Why don't we start a company?" In those days, it cost £100 to start a company. He said, "Do you have 50 quid?" I said yes, so we started Acorn. If it had cost a thousand pounds, we might not have started it.

Hermann Hauser, entrepreneur and investor

Others have simply followed an idea that set them on the path to founding a company because it was the only way the idea could come to fruition.

When we started working on what became Simprints, I never thought we'd build a company. I attended a hackathon in 2012 that was looking at how to improve the way we deliver digital healthcare in developing countries, and that was where the first idea of using biometrics came from...We started working on this as a nights and weekends project...I had no ambition whatsoever to be an entrepreneur, to actually build a company.

Toby Norman, entrepreneur

Others are even more fuzzy about how it began, but once they started on the journey, they seized the opportunity with both hands.

> I wasn't really thinking about starting a company. That kind of happened to me.
>
> Dominic Hill, entrepreneur

Whether you're an accidental entrepreneur – like Toby, Hermann or Dominic – or you've always wanted to start a business ever since you were a child, we hope you'll find some useful lessons and ideas in this book. It is packed with stories and advice from entrepreneurs who are just starting out on their first business, those who have set up several businesses, and others who have focused on growing businesses as an investor. All the contributors are listed at the back of the book. Not all of them have recorded podcasts, but many of them have, so if you want to know more about a particular story, go to www.investedinvestor.com and see if their podcast has been published.

If this book helps you make a better-informed decision about whether or not to become an entrepreneur, gives you a good insight into the challenges you will face and how other entrepreneurs have tackled them, and shows you how the various players in the start-up ecosystem can work best together, we'll have done our job. Then it's up to you. Good luck!

> It's great to dream about success. You have to work really hard to actually make it happen. Don't just dream about it. Get on and make it happen.
>
> Gonçalo de Vasconcelos, entrepreneur

CHAPTER 2

Are you an entrepreneur?

6   I get out of bed in the morning to change the world.

Before you set up and run a business, you must ask yourself the very basic question, 'Should I be an entrepreneur at all?' It's not an easy question to answer. Don't assume that working for yourself is the right way to go just because you don't like working for someone else.

Any internet search for successful entrepreneurs will bring up a variety of people who don't appear to share many defining characteristics. Bridge-playing computer guy Bill Gates is not the same type of person as kite-surfing record-stores-to-spaceflight billionaire Richard Branson, who in turn is very different from airline founder Michael O'Leary, and none of them bear much resemblance to lingerie titan Michelle Mone. But delve a little deeper, and you do find some fundamental similarities that hint at how they've managed to be so successful. They have all made sacrifices, they have all worked extremely hard, they have learned from their mistakes and, in the long run, they have proved resilient in the face of numerous difficulties and challenges.

The phrase 'know thyself' – supposedly inscribed above the entrance to the Temple at Delphi, home to the famous oracle – is particularly apposite if you're thinking about becoming an entrepreneur. Do you have the right traits? Can you be humble when you don't know it all? Can you be honest with yourself about what you do and don't know, what you can and can't do? Are you willing to learn? Are you resilient? Are you willing to work hard and make sacrifices? More than 50% of start-ups fail – how will you cope if that happens to you? And then, on the upside, what will success look like for you? How will you measure it?

In this chapter, we hear about the personal qualities that help entrepreneurs to succeed, and the sacrifices they have to make as they launch themselves into the unknown. Some of our entrepreneurs relished the challenge of proving the nay-sayers wrong, or recognised that losing their formerly affluent lifestyle gave them the drive to succeed all over again. Others found that they had an inner fortitude which meant they could get through anything. Above all, they weren't afraid of hard work because, as Gonçalo de Vasconcelos, co-founder of SyndicateRoom says, 'The journey's far tougher than anyone will tell you.'

> From the outside, most people think, "Wow, you run a start-up, that's cool." It's not cool. It's extremely hard and deeply unglamorous work.
>
> **Adam Cleevely, entrepreneur and investor**

Know thyself

> ❝ I didn't figure out I could be entrepreneurial until I was 39 or 40.
>
> Jon Bradford, entrepreneur and investor

It sounds obvious, but it's essential to be honest with yourself if you're thinking of starting a business, and being honest includes really understanding your own ambitions, character and strengths. You have to take a long hard look at yourself and decide what you are willing to do and sacrifice to make your dream a reality.

> ❝ I think I'm entrepreneurial, but I'm not sure I'm a founder.
>
> Gemma Milne, journalist

We're not all cut out to be entrepreneurs. Sometimes it's simply because we're not in a position to take the necessary risks – a new mortgage or a young family might mean the entrepreneurial journey has to be put on hold for now. Or perhaps you might, like Gemma Milne or Tomi Davies, come to the conclusion that you have a different role to play.

> ❝ I started out as a software programmer, from COBOL to FORTRAN, PL/1, ALGOL…So I think I've always seen myself as a technology person. But when I really look at it, it's been business…I am your number two man in a team. I am a team player. I do run my consultancy, but I've never seen myself as the lead man. Yet I've played on some very powerful teams.
>
> Tomi Davies, investor

However, for some entrepreneurs, life is barely worth living if they're not following their dream. And that dream may last a very long time – Lord Karan Bilimoria co-founded Cobra Beer in 1989, and by 2014, apart from its international sales, Cobra's market share of licensed Indian restaurants in the UK was around 98%. But for Lord Bilimoria, the adventure is still fresh.

> ❝ Authentic entrepreneurs are passionate about what they do. They really love their business, their brand, their product. To this day, I cannot go into a supermarket without checking the Cobras and rearranging the shelves.
>
> Lord Bilimoria, entrepreneur

If you can recognise your own motivations and limitations, then you are on the way to possessing what investor Ramona Liberoff sees as two key traits of successful entrepreneurs – to be both humble and visionary. The vision is what gives you the drive to build a business, but being humble means that you will constantly benchmark your skillset against what is best for the company, and bring in the right people and advice to cover the areas where you are lacking. That in turn helps you to build the trust and transparency that creates a virtuous circle to drive the business forward.

> ❝ I think the most important thing is to try and learn from other people's mistakes. I want other people to learn from my mistakes, and I'm very happy to try and help people to do that... There's this joke in Cambridge that you're never more than one pint away from the answer to any problem...I'm often surprised how generous people are in helping you if you've got a problem.
>
> Pilgrim Beart, entrepreneur

Why is it so important to understand yourself and to ask for help when you need it? Leaders who do not acknowledge and address their own failings often find themselves leading a failing business.

Are you willing to learn?

One of the key questions to ask yourself is, are you willing to learn? All of the entrepreneurs we spoke to highlighted the need to listen and learn – essential skills for the first-time entrepreneur, for whom everything is new, but also for those on the second and third time around. Their earlier experiences will have taught them a lot, but there are still plenty of surprises, even for the most seasoned entrepreneurs. And things change: when Sir Richard Branson founded Virgin Records back in 1972, we were buying vinyl singles and LPs; today, the Virgin Group is global, and the brand encompasses everything from telecommunications to space travel, using technologies that hadn't been invented when Branson started his entrepreneurial career.

> I was incredibly lucky to be surrounded by people who have been there and done it, and if they had any tips, it would be silly of me not to listen.
>
> Gonçalo de Vasconcelos, entrepreneur

You must not only be willing to learn, but also understand that learning is hard work. Sometimes there is so much to take in that you might feel overwhelmed. At other times, it is the learning that keeps you going.

> There's never an end to learning and every day in a start-up is a learning experience. It is also challenging to be learning every day, and exhausting to be learning every day...You flip between being excited about the thing you've just learned to being annoyed by something you don't know how to do.
>
> Fiona Nielsen, entrepreneur

As well as learning about the nuts and bolts of starting and running a business, entrepreneurs must also be ready to learn about themselves and use that experience to grow and develop their skills. Pilgrim Beart and Victor Christou both did this, but for different reasons and from very different perspectives. For Pilgrim, his growing self-awareness had to come the hard way.

> People sometimes ask me what my lessons from [the failure] were, but they were so numerous, I hardly know where to start. In retrospect, I now realise I was an R&D engineer...I'd gone up the management ladder and started to understand how teams work, and how products are defined and so on.

> But I really had had no exposure at all to the big picture of companies, boards, investors, and a lot of detailed customer engagement. And I had to try and learn all of that quickly.
>
> Pilgrim Beart, entrepreneur

Victor Christou had been part of creating one company as a 'technologist', as he explained, but nevertheless felt that he didn't know enough about business and needed to expand his knowledge and skills if he was going to do it again. So he headed to Stanford to take an MBA. He thought he'd learn the practical, process side of business – accounts, corporate finance, economics, and so on – but ended up learning a lot more than the basic ingredients of corporate life.

> The most important things I learned in Stanford were things I discounted initially…The most transformative classes I took were interpersonal classes…It's interesting being exposed to your own vulnerabilities and blind spots. It's not about you dealing with your own issues, it's about understanding your impact on other people and how other people impact you. It was a revelation.
>
> Victor Christou, entrepreneur and investor

Business is 90% about people, as they say, and Victor recognised that running a business means interacting with people with lots of different needs and lots of different character types. Customers, team members, employees, potential supporters and influencers – they won't all come from the same mould. And being able to empathise, react and respond could be the difference between a successful team and a dysfunctional team.

> If you can help somebody when you sense something's not right in your team, if you can…spot something before it becomes a big issue, you're going to be a lot more successful. You can have the best value proposition in the world and the best technology in the world, but if you haven't got rapport

with people, and you don't really understand how you're influencing them and how you're perceived, and what people are going to do as a result of the interactions with you, then it all kind of falls apart.

Emily MacKay, entrepreneur

Victor's learning from Stanford became even more valuable when he took a class with the chief negotiator of General Motors. The class opened Victor's eyes to the lasting effects of negotiations and the enduring nature of relationships in the business world. A key point was that people who maximise their own position at the expense of others tend to have relatively short careers, whereas those who are prepared to compromise will build relationships that survive. And, as he pointed out, 'Relationships you build early on in your career can come back and have an impact on you later…so you need to think about the way you behave in business.'

If you are good to people, people are good to you. There's this reciprocity that is much more than a theory. You don't have to maximise your own position in order to be successful. Don't always try to get the best price and play a zero-sum game where you have to win and someone else has to lose. There are multiple positions where, if you compromise a bit, all parties can win.

Victor Christou, entrepreneur and investor

Are you resilient?

Nothing had even come close to preparing me for the stress and pressure one faces as an entrepreneur. While anyone can understand that situations such as cashflow issues, HR issues, customer problems, fundraising, technology failures, et cetera, are stressful, it's so difficult to convey how hard it is to deal with this when you are fighting fires day in day out…coupled with the fact that a whole host of people have high expectations for you, be it staff, friends, family, shareholders, customers – and

you can't let them down – the emotional burden founders may
have to carry at times is absolutely immense.

Alex Schey, entrepreneur

We've all heard the expression, 'emotional rollercoaster'. For the
entrepreneur, that particular cliché rings very true. You have so
much invested in your company that the emotions associated with
every event, large or small, good or bad, are magnified. When you
live and breathe your idea, and have persuaded others to join you
on this difficult quest, the burdens on you are immense. Then you
factor in customers, who may be relying on your products for their
own success, and things are magnified even more.

You will experience two feelings while being an entrepreneur. You will fluctuate between euphoria and terror at any
given moment. Hopefully you'll have far more experiences of
euphoria, but you will have moments of terror. This is because
it is your baby…You'll have built this from the ground up, you
have a team…and customers, and when things go wrong, you
take them personally…You go through all sorts of emotions.

Priya Lakhani, entrepreneur

Not only are the consequences of things that happen magnified, but
the speed at which they occur can be a shock. One minute you're
on a steady path to closing some sales, the next minute you've been
thrown off course yet again.

You have to have the stamina to get through all the good and
the bad, particularly the bad. That's what it is to be an entrepreneur. The peaks and troughs are off the scale, sometimes in
the same day or even in the same morning. You feel on top of
the world and the company's going to be a billion-pound company. Then you get an email, or somebody says they're leaving
and then you think, why is this happening to me?

Gonçalo de Vasconcelos, entrepreneur

The biggest challenge to your resilience, of course, will be how you cope with failure.

> I have never failed at so many things as when I've been leading a company. Getting used to failing so, so, SO often is hard, but absolutely necessary. But more important than getting used to it yourself is getting an ever expanding and broader team used to being totally open about their failures. Only by doing so can you build success.
>
> Adam Cleevely, entrepreneur and investor

> I think the key thing about entrepreneurs is that when they get knocked over, they pick themselves up and dust themselves off and get on with it. Everybody's forgotten the two businesses that failed. We remember the one that succeeded, so you've just got to keep going.
>
> Neil McArthur, entrepreneur and investor

Lord Bilimoria, co-founder of Cobra Beer, knows what it's like to nearly lose the business he'd fought for through thick and thin: it's happened more than once.

> I nearly lost my business three times. And the last time – I hope the last time – was in 2009, when we didn't see the financial crisis coming. We didn't see the recession coming. We were a high growth company. We'd been growing for 18 years at 40% compound growth rate per year. And we'd been sacrificing our bottom line for growth and building value in the brand. And suddenly all that growth had zero value and cash not just became king, it became emperor.
>
> Lord Bilimoria, entrepreneur

What Bilimoria recognised was that it wasn't only the financial crisis that almost destroyed his business. He also acknowledged that his own mistakes had contributed to the problems.

> ❝ I made a mistake. I'd hired the wrong team. We were too highly geared, we had too much debt, and we were forced to put the company up for sale in the worst climate you can imagine. And it took almost a year, from 2008 when Lehman's went bust until May 2009, when eventually we formed a joint venture with Molson Coors, one of the largest brewers in the world, through a very painful restructuring process.
>
> Lord Bilimoria, entrepreneur

Some entrepreneurs demonstrate greater resilience than others. But you don't have to go to the same lengths as Erin Haf Davies: her remarkable feats of endurance include rowing across both the Atlantic and the Indian oceans, as well as sailing in some of the toughest ocean-going races around. She believes her endurance challenges reflect her tenacity as an entrepreneur.

> ❝ Successfully rowing across an ocean does give you a belief that if you apply yourself, then you can go out and achieve anything...I think it's to do with demonstrating that if I start something, I really try and follow it through to the end... Rowing an ocean, you're broken, a storm comes and hits you, you really need to want to be there. I guess it's the same way at Aparito [her company], when it's not so enjoyable, I remind myself that I really want to be here.
>
> Elin Haf Davies, entrepreneur

Are you willing to make sacrifices?

> ❝ Unless you're at the point where you're willing to give it what it takes, don't even start.
>
> Fiona Nielsen, entrepreneur

We know that entrepreneurs work hard. We also know that they have to make sacrifices in order to get their businesses off the ground. So how far are you willing to go? What are you willing to give up in order to follow your dreams?

> I ate a lot of lentils.
>
> Jelena Aleksic, entrepreneur

Plenty of entrepreneurs will tell you they took no salary, or the bare minimum, while they grew their business. Several of the entrepreneurs in this book didn't pay themselves for the first two years of their new business venture. But sometimes that isn't enough.

> I put my house on the line to get more credit and more runway for the company. That's when you're not only burning bridges, you're digging holes under yourself...I remember cycling everywhere, even from Crouch End to Putney in the rain...I didn't get public transport because I [had to] reduce costs down to zero, and that was the only way to survive at the time.
>
> Dominic Hill, entrepreneur

Jonathan Milner remortgaged the house he had just bought in order to show he had the courage of his convictions. He also resorted to knocking on laboratory doors carrying an ice bucket of samples when things were about as bad as they could get. The company he co-founded, Abcam, has a market capitalization of around £2.5 billion at the time of writing.

For the founders of Opsys, holidays became a thing of the past. Even a wedding couldn't get in the way of selling the business when it came time to exit.

> In the five years we spent creating Opsys, not one of the founders took a holiday, we just worked all the time. All of us were single. One guy actually got married...The run-up to selling the business was the run-up to his wedding. I remember negotiating the sales terms on the day of his wedding ... When you're selling a business, as a founder of the business, nothing is more important...We were all getting changed into our suits for the wedding, trying to negotiate the deal with the lawyers.
>
> Victor Christou, entrepreneur and investor

Ofri Ben-Porat had to move his home from one country to another in order to gain the momentum his business needed. Having started developing the technology in Israel, he found that some of his largest customers were elsewhere.

> I would have a meeting in London, go back to the airport to go to Israel, get an email at the airport from the guy I met saying, "Listen, I pitched you to my boss, the CMO, he loves it. Can you come in tomorrow at 9am?" And I'm already at the airport, flying back to Israel. I'd say, "I'll be back in London next week," but by then the conversation had gone cold.
>
> Ofri Ben-Porat, entrepreneur

Ofri knew that, once the company had secured its next funding round, he would have to move. Once the round closed, he packed up and left his colleagues in Tel Aviv, and set up in a co-working space in London, 'Just me and my laptop,' as he says. But now, he could follow up on promising meetings and keep the conversation going towards a sale, rather than having to make up for lost time each time he returned to Europe.

You might not have to move country, but you might have to live and breathe the business 24 hours a day – almost literally.

> We lived in a roof conversion, on the Fulham Palace Road when I started Cobra. The second floor was my partner's bedroom, my bedroom and the kitchen, and the floor above was the sitting and dining room, which was the office. The dining table was our office table, sitting room where we'd meet people, and we'd carry the beer…up those three flights of stairs and stack a tonne of beer, literally, up the flight of stairs – and then carry it all the way back down to deliver it.
>
> So you wake up and you're at the office table, and you work till late at night and so you give it your everything. There is no time to even think of doing anything else.
>
> Lord Bilimoria, entrepreneur

For Alex Schey, starting a company gave him a masterclass in the importance of work/life balance.

> It's very easy to become totally infatuated with the business and spend all your time on it. It seems like there's such a huge mountain of work to get on with, that you won't get anywhere unless you sacrifice most/all of your personal time. Being able to do this for short periods of time is almost certainly necessary, but over long periods this behaviour will begin to take its toll...it was only recently that I managed to get over the guilt of not putting in a day of work over the weekends. It's really important to remember that the business cannot function well if its staff – including its founders – are not looking after themselves.
>
> Alex Schey, entrepreneur

Can you cope with rejection?

> I want to see that moment when they realise they were wrong.
>
> Dominic Hill, entrepreneur

Are you the sort of person who will crumble when others don't believe in you, or will their negativity spur you on to work even harder to see your idea come to fruition?

> I get out of bed in the morning because I want to change this industry, and I want to see the look in the eyes of all the people who told me that it couldn't be done or that it was a waste of time.
>
> Dominic Hill, entrepreneur

Fiona Nielsen, founder and CEO of Repositive, reckons that, 'If you can't take a "no", you shouldn't start a company.' As a popular speaker for would-be entrepreneurs, she has a simple way of getting her message across.

❝   I often give talks to students, and they come up to me after and say "I want to start a company, it's my big dream. Should I?" I say, "No." And they look shocked, and ask why I tell them not to start a company. I say, "If you can't take a 'no', you shouldn't start a company." You'd better get used to it, because if you want to start a company you need to know – not exactly what you want to do, but you need to be very, very driven by what you want to achieve, because if you don't have a good reason to put all that effort in to it, you're going to hit the first bump on the road and give up.

Fiona Nielsen, entrepreneur

The nay-sayers – Priya's story

I'm going to defy those people and just do it anyway.

Priya Lakhani, entrepreneur

Once you reveal you're thinking about setting up a business, there will be plenty of people who'll say you can't do it, and negative voices from the past may come back to haunt you. But for some entrepreneurs, such negativity is exactly what spurs them on. Priya Lakhani, founder and CEO of Century Tech, is one entrepreneur who won't take 'no' for an answer.

When I wanted to be a lawyer, my head teacher said, "You're never going to be a barrister – you're brown, you're female, you're from an ethnic minority. Barristers tend to be white males who go to Oxbridge, and you're not going to Oxbridge, either."

Priya defied her head teacher and went on to qualify as a libel lawyer and launch a successful career. But that wasn't enough. She knew she wasn't destined to be a lawyer all her life, so she decided to follow her entrepreneurial leanings. Her first company was the successful food brand Masala Masala. She had spotted a gap in the market for fresh ethnic sauces and, despite having no experience in the food industry, believed in her own talents – and her mother's recipes. Plenty of people thought differently.

There are always nay-sayers…There'll always be a small portion of the population who'll say you can't. So, I thought, I'm going to defy those people and just do it anyway…and I really enjoyed the challenge… Within six weeks, I had nationwide supermarket deals.

Priya secured deals not only with major supermarkets such as Waitrose, but also with famous London department stores Harvey Nichols and Harrods. And there was a social angle to her business as well: each pot of sauce sold meant a meal for a homeless person in India. Eventually, this added up to millions of meals, and proceeds also went towards providing some 35,000 vaccinations in Africa and building schools in the most deprived areas.

Circumstances suddenly conspired against her. Illness in her family occurred at the same time as problems developed with Masala Masala's manufacturer and distributor. With a new baby also on the way, Priya reached a point where she had to, as she says, 'press pause' on the business in order to focus on her family.

Nevertheless, her entrepreneurial spirit refused to quieten down and it wasn't long before she found another problem to solve. As an advisor to the UK Government's Department for Business Innovation and Skills, she had begun to look at education. She found that 1.8 million children were underperforming at school, and that teachers were faced with the double burden of large class sizes and equally large amounts of paperwork – up to 60% of teacher time was spent on data entry and admin. This information was put to the back of her mind while she was coping with everything else going on around her, but it led to her next start-up, Century Tech.

Despite the success of Masala Masala, Priya faced opposition once more, this time because of her lack of a technological background. Sometimes, that opposition got heated.

I've been yelled at, shouted at, told I'm not good enough, told to quit, to go home and stop wasting everyone's time.

Priya was determined once more to prove the nay-sayers wrong. Today, Century Tech combines machine learning, big data analytics and cognitive neuroscience to create a technology platform that helps teachers to provide personalised learning for children. So what is Priya's advice to the entrepreneur surrounded by people saying they can't do it?

Ignore the nay-sayers. You're going to get so many of them, and it can be really disheartening, but just ignore them. Follow your gut instincts.

Listen to any advice and ask yourself, "Is there anything useful in this advice that I can take on to make my product better, or my offering better, or to make my deck better?" – but then keep going.

Priya Lakhani, entrepreneur

Taking the plunge – Dominic's story

I knew I had to jump out of the Titanic, but I jumped into a boat that was full of holes.

Dominic Hill, entrepreneur

Deciding you have all the attributes needed to be an entrepreneur – being able to work hard, deal with rejection, cope with failure and make sacrifices, while all the time being emotionally resilient – is all very well, but taking the plunge and making your dream a reality is still a leap into the unknown. Dominic Hill's journey from traditional jewellery wholesaler to eCommerce disrupter illustrates just how dramatic a change it can be to go from a secure job with a very comfortable salary to an uncertain future with no income at all.

I began to feel like I was sitting in a golden cage. I had my sports car. I'd paid for my place in a relatively affluent part of north London, I had a parking space in central London and I was turning left in planes. I felt like I was stagnating, and I didn't know what I wanted to do, but I knew that this wasn't enough or wasn't right for me.

As these feelings were surfacing, Dominic attended a prestigious industry leaders summit in Austria and heard a presentation given by Chris Morton, one of the founders of Lyst.

It was like a big slap around the face that made me think, "I've been asleep." I'd been congratulating myself on what a great job I've been doing and aren't I great? And here's somebody whose trajectory has been completely different to mine. Finding out he was three years younger than me was even more shocking. That was the moment when I knew something needed to change.

Dominic had to trust his instincts. His employers were wedded to their traditional model and not prepared to reinvent themselves to operate in a modern, digital economy, and he realised it was time to leave. But he still wasn't ready to set up on his own and took a job with a start-up that looked perfect on paper.

> *I took a position as a managing director at a young start-up called My Flash Trash, which was run by Amber Atherton, who is extremely intelligent and very successful. The start-up focused primarily on PR. That's where they were making money, but the vision was to make it into this fashion eCommerce pure play for jewellery, and she needed somebody to build that. I had the experience and the contacts and the know-how, and she had the connections and the start-up and the funding. So it seemed like a win-win.*
>
> *Amber is a very dynamic person. She was also very young at the time, 22. I've got a lot of respect for her, but I realised pretty quickly that maybe she wasn't quite ready to have somebody else drive her car. So within six to eight weeks, maybe even less, we amicably agreed that this wasn't going to work out. I didn't leave her in the dumps. I kept on for a couple of months and enabled her to transition out of our agreement, and we're amicable to this day. So it was a bad situation, but we managed our way out of it.*

But now Dominic had completely burned his bridges. The start-up idea hadn't worked, and his one-time dream position with his first company, the position he had left, had already been taken by someone else.

However, he started to put together a few things that had happened in the last weeks at his previous job. At one of the key trade shows in Hong Kong, he'd told a few of his contacts that he was leaving and the responses were striking.

> *I told a couple of people that I was leaving, and they pretty much refused to let me walk out of the booth without agreeing in some way, shape, or form to continue talking to them or working with them, even if it seemed that what I was going to end up doing was not relevant for them.*
>
> *And I had a similar experience with the buying director at a big German retailer. She said, "Maybe you can just consult with me on my digital strategy." And I said, "But I don't know anything about it. That's why I'm leaving this old world of wholesale because I need to learn*

about eCommerce…That is why I'm taking this massive pay cut and huge risk, because I don't know."

So that began as just a conversation…On the airplane on the way back, I remember thinking that people on the supply side and the demand side had asked if there was something I could do for them. And I thought, could I play them off against each other?

Something else happened during this period: Dominic met a potential investor, even though he had nothing to invest in as yet.

Back in England, I met a chap that I'd pitched to previously…and he said, "What are you up to?" I replied, "I've just jumped from the position where I was and I've joined this start-up." At the time, I think he was potentially interested in investing in the start-up, so he asked to remain in contact.

Dominic's original idea, wondering how he could play off buyers against sellers, came from a consultancy mindset; after all, that was what he knew and what he had the contacts to build on. But then he realised that the real issue was a compounding problem – how could buyers and sellers interact in the most efficient and cost-effective way possible? The result was Atelier Technology, the world's first software as a service (SaaS) play in jewellery.

Until you burn your bridges…I mean really burn them until you've got no other option, there's no food on the table….Until you do that, you're not actually going to find your fifth gear, that extra something.

Dominic Hill, entrepreneur

THREE THINGS ABOUT BEING AN ENTREPRENEUR
- Having an idea and turning it into the core of a successful company is very hard work – probably harder than you can imagine.
- Be honest with yourself. Are you resilient? Can you handle failure? Are you open to learning? Can you overcome barriers?
- Only take 'no' for an answer if you believe it is the right answer. Don't be put off by people who don't know the depth of your passion or the strength of your character.

CHAPTER 3

Founder or co-founders?

6 I love him to death and on any given day I might want to kill him.

Who is starting this business? Is it just you, or have you got a colleague or friend who is eager to join you on the adventure? Is there a family member who is convinced you'd make a good team? Perhaps you've been sharing ideas with several other people and have to choose who to stick with. So the first question you have to ask yourself is: do you take the plunge as a sole founder, or do you look for a co-founder? You may have already begun developing your ideas with a colleague or friend, but you have to think hard about whether the two, or more, of you should go into business together. Sometimes it's easier to have an idea than to decide how best to get it off the ground.

Why is the founder/co-founder decision so important?

> ❝ He was brilliant. He did the marketing, the sales, the product conception, and I gathered the team.
>
> Hermann Hauser, entrepreneur and investor

Opinion is divided on whether or not you are wise to start a business on your own. Back in 2016, inventor, investor and TechCrunch writer Haje Jan Kamps claimed that 'more than half of start-ups with an exit did so with just a single founder'. His conclusion was based on several thousand companies registered on Crunchbase. The average number of founders reported across two datasets (companies that had raised more than $10 million and companies that had exited successfully whether or not they had raised $10 million) was 1.72, a drop from 2.09 in a similar study ten years before. Just over 52% of the companies in the successful exit database had only one founder.

Two years later, research from the MIT Sloan School of Management backed this up, pointing to business celebrities such as Jeff Bezos of Amazon and Sara Blakely of Spanx as stellar examples of solo founders. The research itself was based on a large sample of Kickstarter projects launched between 2009 and 2015. However, this meant that many of them had not been going long enough to truly say whether or not they were successful, so perhaps the researchers' claim that 'solo founders are more than twice as likely to own an ongoing, for-profit venture than two or more founders' should be taken with a pinch of salt. And, of course, for every celebrity solo founder, there are plenty of equally famous pairs of founders – think Paul Allen and Bill Gates, Larry Page and Sergey Brin, Steve Jobs and Steve Wozniack.

Despite the evidence supporting solo entrepreneurs, many investors and some accelerators – such as Y Combinator – tend not to accept single founders, or strongly encourage them to find a co-founder as part of the process. Drew Houston applied to Y Combinator as sole founder of his company, but was only accepted on condition that he identified and partnered with a co-founder before he began the programme – in two weeks' time. A friend of a friend suggested MIT student Arash Ferdowsi, and Houston spent two hours persuading Ferdowsi to drop out of college and join him in starting a company he was going to call Dropbox. Ten years later, when Dropbox launched its successful IPO, Ferdowsi joined the college drop-out billionaire club.

One thing the MIT Sloan researchers highlighted was the problems that co-founders can face. In the stressful world of the start-up, disagreements can all too easily flare into conflicts that shake the foundations of the enterprise, and leave the founders wishing they'd set up on their own, or had never bothered in the first place, or, as the researchers state, 'It becomes far from clear that a team is preferable to a solo founder.'

Paul Graham, founder of Y Combinator, claimed that about 20% of the start-ups they funded had a founder leave, but that wasn't always the death knell for the business. It depended on a number of factors, including how many founders there were (for instance, one out of two founders leaving may be harder to deal with than one of three founders leaving), and what skills they took away with them. A founder leaving may signal that they lack the necessary commitment to the business, and that might be a relief.

Indeed, the difficulties encountered by some co-founders are well-documented. Paul Allen left Microsoft, the company he founded with Bill Gates, after seeing his equity squeezed because, as he claimed, others felt he was unproductive – while he was undergoing treatment for cancer. Steve Wozniak left Apple in 1985 because he didn't like the direction the company was going in.

Which might lead you to think that the fairy-tale ending for the Dropbox founders is a fluke and you'd be much better off starting your company on your own. But think again. There are plenty of reasons why a co-founder can make things easier, from having someone to bounce ideas off to bringing complementary skills where you have gaps, and from providing a shoulder to cry on to helping open that celebratory bottle when the first big customer is signed. And investors, despite research like that of TechCrunch and MIT, still prefer to fund co-founders rather than sole founders, because they see few entrepreneurs with the complete skill set needed to set up and run a successful business.

So you have an important decision to make before you've even started on your entrepreneurial adventure. Let's see what some of our entrepreneurs had to say about the tricky business of deciding if they wanted one or more co-founders, and how the situation panned out.

> Being a sole founder is tough!
>
> Adam Kerr, entrepreneur

The sole founder – Priya's story

I'd gone from wearing a three-piece suit as a barrister to wearing a hoodie and jogging bottoms driving a van.

Priya Lakhani, entrepreneur

Being a sole founder means not only that you don't have anyone to share and challenge ideas with, but also that you have to do all the work. You need to be prepared to live and breathe your business to get it off the ground, and that can involve not only learning new skills, but also going to places and doing jobs that are surprisingly different to what you've experienced in the past.

Priya Lakhani, who we met in Chapter 2, had already caught the money-making bug as a child – selling chocolate bars at school and using some of the proceeds to buy shares, with the help of her mother. After training and working as a lawyer, she couldn't resist going back to the entrepreneurial life.

Priya chose the sole founder route, but even she hadn't anticipated how much work would be involved and how much she didn't know about the food industry she was launching into, nor how that would affect people's reactions to her efforts.

> *I had to learn everything, just for the samples. I did a health and safety course, found a company to test our samples for bacteria…Then I had to find a manufacturer…and most of them laughed me out of the door.*

It wasn't only the manufacturers who laughed at Priya. All the suppliers she approached also scoffed at her ambitions to sell in all the big supermarkets when she was all alone and knew so little about the sector. They told her it would be impossible to get in to see the buyers, let alone persuade them that a small company could provide the quantities they would need.

Priya could have chosen to partner with someone more familiar with the food industry and selling into supermarkets, and that might have made things easier. On the other hand, her lack of knowledge might have been behind her success. Someone with sector experience might have been more cautious due to previous knock-backs. They might well have persisted with trying the more well-worn routes into big supermarket chains and acted as a dampener to Priya's enthusiasm.

Priya's determination and audacity paid off. Masala Masala went on to be a major success, with 11,000 Waitrose and Ocado customers rating the sauces as excellent or very good. Priya's words of wisdom for entrepreneurs who want to go it alone?

> *When things go wrong, you will take it personally…If that doesn't feel comfortable, then you're better off finding an entrepreneurial company to work in where you're not the founder.*

> Priya Lakhani, entrepreneur

The accidental sole founder – Elin's story

> *I never actually planned to start my own company.*

> Elin Haf Davies, entrepreneur

It sounds strange, but some entrepreneurs really do end up founding a company without actually setting out to do so. In these cases, the founder or co-founders question might never come up.

Dr Elin Haf Davies is one such case. She trained as a paediatric nurse, mostly caring for children with rare diseases, and then moved into researching how children that were recruited into clinical trials were looked after. She subsequently went to work for what was then known as the European Medicine Evaluation Agency after the EU introduced regulations which obliged pharmaceutical companies to consider the needs of children during drug development – what Elin describes as the concept that 'it's more ethical to protect children through research than to protect children from research'.

Eventually, she found herself leading part of a WHO working group looking at essential medicines for children, but became very frustrated that the changes she wanted to see in clinical trials weren't happening. She thought of going back into academia and research, but recognised that that route would still be too restrictive. If she was going to work towards promoting the changes she wanted to see in the way she wanted to do it, Erin needed to operate under a legal entity, and so she registered her company, Aparito, purely as a vehicle for her activities.

But that route turned out to be key: Erin was approaching the problem from the side of patient need and the clinical perspective, instead of developing a technology and then seeing if there was a problem it might solve. She was painfully aware that most medical trials only captured a small amount of data on the patient's responses – the information provided when the patient visited hospital for a check-up. She believed that there was a way to develop remote, real-time monitoring that would capture much greater amounts of useful data, but which did not involve creating an entirely new technology. Better patient information could bring major improvements to drug trials and treatment regimes, and Aparito morphed into a company with a solution to the problem.

Nevertheless, Elin had some challenges to overcome once she realised she was founding a business. Going through two investment rounds was a culture shock, as she learned how few female entrepreneurs there were in the med-tech digital health space. Her lack of corporate or industry background also meant that many assumed she was trying to set up a charity or non-governmental organisation rather than a company.

> *It was quite difficult to stick to saying what I wanted to achieve and not change the pitch to suit what investors seemed to want to hear.*
>
> Elin Haf Davies, entrepreneur

The investors that came on board were able to help Elin understand the space, and her healthcare background gave her a unique understanding of how technology could best serve the end purpose of helping patients. It also gave her the drive and determination to keep going even when things were taking longer than expected. And, like so many of our founders, she didn't take any salary for the first two years.

Choosing your co-founders

> Just because you're a mate, you've been to the pub every Friday for the last three years, doesn't make you a good co-founder.
>
> Jon Bradford, entrepreneur and investor

Co-founders come together for all sorts of reasons. They might be old friends, former colleagues, fellow team members on a project, or relatives. They could find each other through networking meetings arranged for people in their sector, or accidentally at a social event. However they find each other, co-founders have a lot to think about as they decide if they should go into business together.

Some entrepreneurs try to go it alone and then admit that they need a co-founder to share the load.

> In the early days of Echion, I was dealing with the downward portion of the Dunning-Kruger curve on my own. Things got much better and [more] enjoyable as soon as I found my full-time co-founder. In retrospect, it probably would have been best to find a co-founder first, and then move full-time to developing an idea into a company.
>
> Jean de La Verpilliere, entrepreneur

The Dunning-Kruger effect is related to our understanding of our own skills – whether we think we are competent even if we are not. Various graphic representations show how an individual's confidence falls as they gain experience and realise their skills or knowledge are not as expert as they believed, or that they simply can't do everything themselves, which is why Jean de La Verpilliere brought in Alex Groombridge to be co-founder and Chief Technology Officer.

As we've seen, Priya Lakhani approached this issue by knowing from the outset that she would have a lot to learn, since she was going into a completely new sector that couldn't be more different from the legal profession which had been her career to date. She was ready to be ignorant and ready to learn. More likely sufferers of the Dunning-Kruger effect are those who think they are expert in their field, and then find that, perhaps, being a leading researcher doesn't automatically translate into being a leading entrepreneur as well.

Others might make the strategic decision to wait a while before they bring in a co-founder, so that they have a clearer understanding of what they need that person to bring to the table. That was the route Gonçalo de Vasconcelos, co-founder of SyndicateRoom, took. He planned to work on his idea and get it as developed as he could on his own before bringing in a co-founder. This not only gave him time to really understand what it was he wanted to do, but also meant that he developed a clearer idea of the profile he should look for in a co-founder.

> My co-founder, Tom Britton, actually joined me about a year and a half after I had started working on my idea. I met Tom through business school – he did the same MBA programme as me, a couple of years after I had finished. I had already sorted out the legal issues and the basics of the technology.
>
> Gonçalo de Vasconcelos, entrepreneur

It turned out that Gonçalo had made a wise choice, as Tom's start at the company didn't quite go as planned – he was fired on his first day.

> I had raised two family and friends rounds to get to that point, and was about to sign off on another funding round, so

> I expected to have the cash to pay him a salary. That funding round collapsed at the last minute. I had to fire Tom on his first day in the office and then ask him to work for free. He's still with me six years later.
>
> Gonçalo de Vasconcelos, entrepreneur

For others, the co-founder relationship might seem pre-ordained. Jonathan Milner had inklings that he wanted to start a business, but had no idea how to go about it. He met entrepreneur David Cleevely at a dinner party, and it turned out to be a perfect match.

> Jonathan and I had a conversation over dinner…and that conversation was between somebody who was a researcher and was fed up with the quality of antibodies, and somebody who had developed a whole load of web technology and run a business. Jonathan knew how antibodies got produced, I didn't. I understood from talking to him what the economics of antibodies were…and I remember saying to him, "There must be something wrong here. You can't ship these out of the laboratory." And he said, "Oh no, you can seal it in an envelope and they'll survive two, three, four days in the post." I went, "Bloody hell, we've got a business."
>
> David Cleevely, entrepreneur and investor

David became a slightly unusual co-founder, in that his contribution was to spend hours mentoring Jonathan and helping him tackle each stage of the business journey, rather than being hands-on day-to-day, but the arrangement paid off.

We were childhood friends – Lord Bilimoria's story

Lord Bilimoria founded Cobra Beer with his business partner, Arjun Reddy, in 1989. He spotted a gap in the market for the type of lager that went well with Indian food and ended up creating a global brand. Bilimoria and Reddy were particularly close before they went into business, which was the foundation of their success.

Our families had known each other in Hyderabad for four generations. My mother was at school with his mother, my grandmother was at school with his grandmother, our great-grandparents knew each other, and so on. So there was immediate trust, and I think it's so important in partnerships, in business... Trust is the essence.

Lord Bilimoria, entrepreneur

Despite planning to eventually brew and sell beer, they took the slightly unusual route of selling some completely different products first in order to build their business experience. But having a co-founder doesn't make life easier: now you're both working hard, especially if you both still have day jobs.

He was working during the day, I was working during the day, and we'd meet up in the evenings to work on our own business. For the first nine months, we built up experience importing products from India and selling them over here... Selling, marketing, procurement, production, we got experience. The beer was a big idea but we weren't ready for the big idea. We needed time for that and we had to learn.

Our first venture was importing polo sticks from Kolkata in India. For my first business deal, I managed to sell hundreds of sticks to a saddler I used to play against. We had lunch in Fulham at the Pigeon Restaurant, and he gave me half the money up front, and that was my working capital. I put my order in to the stick makers in Kolkata and I was in business.

Lord Bilimoria, entrepreneur

Everybody else left – Jelena's story

What if you have no choice? There are cases where the founders happen to be the only ones willing to pursue an idea. Jelena Aleksic ended up as a co-founder because she and her colleague, Robert Stojnic, were the last two standing.

Jelena and Robert co-founded Gene Adviser, a company set up to bring the benefits of new techniques in data analysis and bioinformatics to healthcare providers. Jelena had already been involved in a couple of other start-ups alongside her full-time job, but this was the first time she was going to put all her time and resources into a company.

As with so many start-ups, the ideas had been gestating for a while among Jelena and some of her colleagues, but when it came to the crunch, they didn't have the same appetite for risk, as Jelena explains.

> In the very early stages, there was a group of us who were friends, and we were entering business competitions for fun. That lets you play around with ideas, and we won a few competitions and went out for dinner on the proceeds. Tweaking the idea led more and more to something that really looked like a business. It came to the stage where we sat down and had the conversation of, "Sure, we can do this. Who wants to stay?" At that point, everybody else left.
>
> Jelena Aleksic, entrepreneur

One colleague, Robert, remained, and the two decided to become business partners, but they didn't jump ship right away.

> Going through that process is scary, and you're stepping away from what you've always been told will be success in your profession...It took about a year and a half [to develop the idea] while we still had full-time employment and an income.
>
> Jelena Aleksic, entrepreneur

Coping with financial uncertainty is an issue for many. Jelena and Robert did a considerable amount of market research and secured a contract before they raised their first funding round, which gave them the confidence to take the plunge. They joined an accelerator programme and then two incubators, which brought them advice, free office space and mentoring. But it didn't bring them any money to start with, so they lived off savings and a small amount of grant funding.

As we saw in Chapter 2, this meant Jelena had to cut back on everything but the essentials, including food – as she says, she ate a lot of lentils. But having the decision about co-founders essentially made for you could end up being a good thing. When people rule themselves out, you know they don't have the passion or the appetite for risk that the start-up will need. Or perhaps they just hate lentils.

Making the co-founder relationship work

A co-founder relationship can be difficult, to say the least. Starting a company is highly stressful and very hard work. There are all sorts of opportunities for things to get heated when the strategy isn't going to plan or an unexpected glitch throws a spanner in the works.

Co-founders will be passionate about the business and the vision, but as they grow and gain experience, they may well have differing opinions on how that vision should be delivered.

> Know your co-founders. Don't let things get into such a state that you can't talk…There are always points in relationships where you can choose whether they turn nasty or not. Sometimes, silence and a good night's sleep is a better solution than anger.
>
> Modwenna Rees-Mogg, entrepreneur and investor

Entrepreneurs need a critical friend. Someone who won't just say 'yes' to all their crazy ideas. Someone who has their best interests at heart but isn't afraid to challenge. That critical friend may be a co-founder as well, which makes it all the more important to have a strong relationship.

> God syndrome is a huge problem. You need to understand that it's inevitable. If you are an entrepreneur and you are successful, it's almost impossible not to suffer from it. But you need to deal with it. My advice is that everyone needs someone to bring them back to earth again.
>
> Carlos Diniz, entrepreneur

Jon Bradford agrees that difference combined with compatibility is crucial.

> You need someone who is willing to be pushy and challenging and sometimes the things you're not. Sean Kane, my co-founder at F6S, is sort of everything I'm not. I love him to

death and on any given day I might want to kill him. We've had real struggles and problems along the way, but we've ended up being stronger because of it and we're thinking of the right things for the business because of it. But we've also had to learn to deal with each other. That equally applies to Sean having to deal with me because I'm a royal pain in the ass.

Jon Bradford, entrepreneur and investor

Ofri Ben-Porat believes a co-founder who shares the business 50-50 is essential, as those brought in at co-founder level and given some shares aren't distinguished enough from an employee with a few shares in their benefits package. With a 50-50 relationship, the burden can be shared equally between the co-founders if the parameters are set at the beginning – a lesson that Ofri has learned.

My relationship with my current co-founder came from a previous venture where we did go 50-50, but where we didn't define exactly who was responsible for what. He, being a very high level professor of maths, was dealing with marketing and business, and I was getting tips on the way we should develop the tech, which I shouldn't [have been doing]…A part of the reason we failed last time was because of that.

Ofri Ben-Porat, entrepreneur

As a result, one of the first conversations the two had when they were thinking about starting another business was about who did what.

I do business, he does tech, and we don't interfere. That doesn't mean we don't talk; we speak every day, more than I speak to my wife. It means no interfering on the decision-making process. There's a saying in the business: "Nadav doesn't speak to people, Ofri doesn't speak to computers, and they have a beautiful, frictionless relationship."

Ofri Ben-Porat, entrepreneur

Sometimes the distinctions between co-founders are not so clear-cut, but that, too, can work.

> ❝ Chris [Curry] and I made all the decisions. I can't remember whether I was chairman and he was managing director or the other way around, and it didn't really matter because we always shared an office. We always listened to what the other person said on the phone. It was an amazingly harmonious relationship.
>
> Hermann Hauser, entrepreneur and investor

All these different co-founder relationships show that your decision has to be made based on your situation and your gut feelings. Just don't forget to do a skills analysis to make sure you're a good fit for the business as well as a good fit for each other.

Two's company, three's a crowd...but four? – Toby's story

Generally, investors say they prefer two or three co-founders. They tend not to like a sole founder for reasons we've already mentioned. Two can work well, and so can three as long as two of the trio don't gang up on the other co-founder if things start to go badly.

Four co-founders is unusual – some investors believe that, by the time you get to four co-founders, some of the skills will be duplicated, and this can give rise to differences of opinion over how to do things.

But having four co-founders works for Simprints. Although several other people were involved in the early days of the project that led to the company being set up, four co-founders had emerged by the time things got serious. Even more unusually, the four were still together five years later, working hard to build their technology and get it out to where it can make a difference.

Toby Norman, one of the co-founders, was all set to go to McKinsey when he had finished his PhD, but found himself heading down a different path.

I attended a hackathon about how we deliver digital healthcare in developing countries, and that was where the idea of using biometrics came from. We started working on it at nights and weekends. After a couple of rounds of co-founders, the final co-founding "class" was four of us, but initially I never thought we'd build a company. I had accepted a job with McKinsey and had no ambition whatsoever to be an entrepreneur.

Toby Norman, entrepreneur

Toby and his friends were working on using biometrics to provide a unique link between a patient and their medical records. Fingerprints were the best choice as a biometric identifier for various reasons, not least because they were the most culturally acceptable in the communities the team wanted to reach. But one of the challenges they discovered was that fingerprint accuracy for those communities was much lower than in more developed countries. They found that farmers and others doing manual work had fingerprints that were worn and scarred, as did women who had spent their lives cooking over open fires.

As we got further and further into this problem, it just became too interesting to let go – and too important to let go. At the end of my PhD, I had to sit down and figure out what I wanted to do next.
It became clear to me that the right thing to do was to turn down the job at McKinsey and throw my weight behind trying to build a tech company to solve this challenge.

By this point, Toby and two friends from Cambridge University – engineer, materials and nanotech specialist Alexandra Grigore, and medical sciences PhD Daniel Storisteanu – had been joined by Toby's brother, Tristram, who had just finished a master's degree in computer science at the University of London. They realised that the only way to address the fingerprint accuracy problem was to hand-collect enough samples to identify the best technologies to work with, but they had almost no resources and had to do everything themselves.

It amounted to hundreds of hours sitting in vaccination clinics, schools, hospitals – myself and my co-founding team taking people's fingers and manually placing them on different types of biometric sensors to figure out which type of hardware and software would give us the best accuracy.

In the end, the team collected some 135,000 fingerprints from four different countries and were able to use their dataset to optimise the hardware and software they were working with. The uplift in accuracy was astonishing: their technology was 228% more accurate than the next best on the market, and their collection is still the world's largest academic dataset of fingerprints from those populations.

It was an incredible amount of effort, but...this is what it took to understand how to make fingerprint technology work in the last mile of healthcare delivery.

Toby Norman, entrepreneur

Not surprisingly, all those hours of effort by the founding four created strong bonds between them and a strong understanding of what they were trying to overcome. They also created a story that continues to impact on the culture of the company, as we shall see in the next chapter.

THREE THINGS ABOUT FOUNDER VS CO–FOUNDERS

- The co-founder relationship is intense, and you will probably spend more time with your co-founder(s) than with your family, so choose wisely.
- Investors might not fund sole founders because they consider putting funding into one person to be inherently riskier than investing in a company with two or three co-founders.
- Very few companies work well with four or more founders, although there are always exceptions to the rule.

CHAPTER 4

Building the team in the early days

> 6 People are hard to manage and entrepreneurs are not very good at that, especially if a team member doesn't think like they do.

Around 75% of the active, early-stage entrepreneurs we polled for this book cited building the team as one of their three biggest challenges. We weren't surprised. It is crucial to get the core team right, as it sets so many of the parameters for the company going forward, and mistakes can be very costly. Putting together a winning team that has the right mix of skills and passion can make the difference between securing investment or running out of cash before the business gets off the ground.

Starting any kind of business is very hard to do on your own, particularly in the technology sector where many of our entrepreneurs come from. Some skills may be transferable, but others have to be added. So even if you have more than one co-founder, you will probably still need to build a core team from the beginning. But how do you gather the right skills? And how do you know what skills you need at each phase of the journey? What do you do if you know what you need, but you don't have the money, or the credibility, to hire the right person?

Then there are the problems that come with any growing company. Inevitably, some hires won't work. What if someone turns out to be a bad fit? How do you make sure everyone is aligned? How do you create the right culture among the team? And how do you fire the people who aren't aligned, or are holding everyone back?

Finding the right people with the right skills and experience to come on the journey with you can be extremely difficult for all sorts of reasons. And to make it more difficult, as you grow the company, you inevitably grow the number of people involved – from just a few of you in the early days, to adding a Board and investors as the company becomes more established, to perhaps adding some specialist advisors, more employees, and, of course, your customers.

More people equal more opportunities for misalignment or a faltering culture, which is why it is so important to get things right from the start. It's a universal problem for entrepreneurs, and there are no simple answers.

> I think there is no formulaic way of doing it. It is a very "human" thing.
>
> Jean de La Verpilliere, entrepreneur

The core team

> Starting a company involves founders wearing a huge number of different hats, and the business is dependent on the founder(s) physically doing a wide range of different tasks. Often, there's simply no-one else to do it, especially in the early days. This makes you busy, but it narrows perspective and can contribute to you not being able to see the wood for the trees.

> To develop and maintain that long-term clarity of vision and think strategically is very important for the business's success, but incredibly challenging to achieve as an entrepreneur – at least until you've scaled and hired a strong, supportive team to take the day-to-day pressure off.
>
> Alex Schey, entrepreneur

The core team is critical. It sets the agenda, creates the culture and provides the drive and passion that are the cornerstones of a successful company. Lord Bilimoria cites the loyalty of his team as one of the three things that helped the company survive when crisis hit – along with the strength of the brand and the support of his wife.

One of the make-or-break factors for the core team is alignment. Does everyone share the same vision and passion for the idea and the company, or are there people who are in it for the wrong motives?

> So much of what goes wrong with start-ups and management teams…can be attributed to the dynamic with the people involved.
>
> One of the biggest things that splits up a founding team is when there is a difference in integrity or a difference in values between the members of that team. That's an absolute disaster.
>
> Ramona Liberoff, entrepreneur and investor

Alignment among the core team is not just about having everybody pointing in the same direction. Victor Christou believes that transparency about motivation is just as important, if not more so: if everyone is transparent about what they are bringing and what they want to get out of the journey, there are fewer unpleasant surprises along the way.

> When you go into a business, be clear with each other about what you want to get out at the end, as you may all have different agendas. One person might decide that their journey with the start-up is done, and if they've been clear about what they

> wanted to get out of it from the start, there are no surprises
> and no one has let anyone down.
>
> Victor Christou, entrepreneur and investor

Different agendas could mean that some team members want to
build a landmark business, while others might want to make a certain amount of money or simply just have the experience of going
through the start-up process. As long as everyone is clear, then no
one can complain when one of the team meets their personal goal
and moves on.

> ❝ As long as you're clear when you want to jump off the bus,
> then no one can complain when you do.
>
> Victor Christou, entrepreneur and investor

What if you've never hired anybody before?

It's all very well saying that the core team and early hires are crucial,
but if you've never hired someone before, how on earth do you go
about such an important task?

Some investors will help with your early hiring decisions. They
know you don't have the experience and will do what they can to
make the process work.

Luke Hakes points out that one of the first priorities is to understand the core functions of a team and what is needed for the business. He finds that, sometimes, the entrepreneurs he works with
claim they don't need a particular function – a CFO for instance
– when Luke and the other investors can see that it's time to fill
that post. Instead of pushing back and insisting, Luke finds that
introducing the founders to other CFOs allows them to learn more
about what the role involves and what it could do for the company.

> ❝ Very quickly, the entrepreneurs go, "Oh wow, I didn't realise
> that person could do those kind of things for me." All of a
> sudden, it goes from a conversation of, "Why do I need that
> person?" to, "How can I find them?"
>
> Luke Hakes, investor

He likes to introduce his entrepreneurs to 'world class examples of whatever the function is' so that they can learn from the best. A mentor in the space can advise not only on what sort of person to look for to match the particular stage of the company, but also what kind of questions to ask in the interview to help identify the right candidate.

> ❦ If you're going to hire a CFO, why not go and find three or four world-class CFOs and ask what questions you should be asking and how you should be hiring a CFO?
>
> Luke Hakes, investor

Asking an expert what they would ask themselves in an interview can be very revealing and very helpful. It's then a question of making sure everyone who will be conducting interviews knows what to ask – and in the early days, that will probably be everyone on the team.

> ❦ It's about helping entrepreneurs understand what good looks like. That's the challenge. If somebody has never hired a team before, they can go and hire a team. But is it a good team? If you don't know what "good" looks like, in a whole host of functions that you've never had any experience with, you're never going to hire the best team.
>
> Luke Hakes, investor

What if you don't have a guiding hand like Luke to help? There are plenty of pitfalls waiting for you, from how and where to find people, to what you can and can't ask in an interview.

For instance, a lot of research shows that diversity in a team improves creativity and problem-solving, and that diverse teams deliver better results, so you have to be very conscious of how and why you make your hiring decisions. It's all too easy to pick people you get on with, and although that's often an essential part of the mix, it could mean you end up hiring people with the same background and skill set as you and fail to create a diverse team that fills in all the gaps.

> We hired a team that was pretty much like us. So at one point, our entire team was made up of PhDs and that felt great. It was a really passionate team, everybody was dedicated to the company mission, but in hindsight, admin support earlier would have been good. You'd assume you'd do anything to have [someone with] a PhD, but you have to build up the capacity the company needs gradually, and when the company needs it. Some more commercial expertise would have been really good.
>
> Jelena Aleksic, entrepreneur

Another aspect that some find difficult is identifying what you cannot do and therefore what you must look for in a new team member. None of us like to admit that we are lacking, and even though you might have a wide range of skills, you have to remember there are only 24 hours in the day and you have to spend a few of those asleep, so you won't be able to do everything yourself.

You have to do some soul-searching and carefully assess and analyse your own skills and experience. It could be a good idea to get some outside help. A coach might help you to look dispassionately at your own CV, and might even help you to identify some skills that you didn't know you had.

Once you've done this, with or without a coach, you should have a clearer picture of what the gaps are and which ones should be filled first. For instance, you may well need someone with product development skills on board full-time from the early days, but accounting could be outsourced while the finances are still relatively straightforward.

> Tom and I, neither of us had any experience in hiring – or firing, for that matter – when we started. The first person we ever interviewed was Fran. She ended up being our first hire. I still remember vividly that we asked Fran, "Explain in your own words what SyndicateRoom does." And she explained it to us in such a way that Tom and I looked at each other and we both thought exactly the same thing, which was, "I wish I had

taken notes to put that on our website." It was a phenomenal explanation. Fran is still with us, and practically a co-founder because she came in so early.

Gonçalo de Vasconcelos, entrepreneur

One thing that often surprises entrepreneurs is just how long it takes to bring new people into the company. It's not just finding them, interviewing them and then negotiating their remuneration package. They will also need some sort of induction and possibly training when they arrive, and this has to be factored into decisions. Time and money constantly have to be balanced in the start-up world.

Going from two to eight full-time in three months after receiving seed funding was challenging. It was a very busy time anyway, and recruiting, onboarding and training new employees takes time and effort. It's not easy to get it right in terms of what mindset, values, etc., to look for when recruiting or to develop when onboarding.

Jean de la Verpilliere, entrepreneur

Expanding the team as the company grows

As your business develops and the core team gets busier and busier, there will come a point when you have to expand the team in order to cope with the workload, or to fill a gap because you get to the point where you, for instance, need a sales manager. But this is often a problem in the early days because there simply isn't enough cash to attract the calibre of person you need.

Some companies get around the salaries problem by hiring people in countries where wages are lower. Jelena and Robert of Gene Adviser found they couldn't afford to hire developers in the UK, and ended up with one member of staff based in Serbia and another in Morocco. The downside of this is the time spent on Skype and travelling to manage a dispersed team, but if it means your technical problems get solved at a lower overall cost, then that helps your funding to go further. Another way to attract the right staff is by having a mission that they feel passionate about, and this can also be important for investors, who look on it as a strength that will help a start-up build a good team.

> In a very early-stage business, you can't hope to pay high quality people the kind of salaries they're going to get elsewhere, so they've got to be on board for the excitement and the vision... Vision and changing the world, or having a view as to how the world can be a better place, is really important for me when I'm thinking about an investment.
>
> Victor Christou, entrepreneur and investor

An associated issue is how you persuade someone to leave a steady job and take the risk of joining a start-up.

> When we were in our Oxford office, we did a memorable interview...with a bright Cambridge engineer who left in dismay after realising we were not a "proper" company!
>
> Sam Cockerill, entrepreneur

The skills a company requires expand and change as it gets bigger, and this will almost certainly impact on how you find and recruit new staff. Initially, you might be focused on developing the product, and most hires will be made with that in mind. Hermann Hauser, co-founder of Acorn computers, found it easy to start with, as he had a ready supply of computer graduates keen to join his company.

> I scoured the university for the best people and...it was so easy because Acorn Computers produced the product that the people I hired actually dreamt of...I never became a computer expert, because I always hired people who were so much smarter than me that I could never catch up with them.
>
> Hermann Hauser, entrepreneur and investor

But as the product is defined and a market fit is established, you will have to find ways to reach beyond the core team's network and into areas and sectors where perhaps you have few, if any, contacts. You will also need to consider how you assess people who will bring expertise that you perhaps don't have any direct experience of or fully understand.

> Initially, it was very easy to find people because my co-founder Adrian and I found a lot of the people we needed from our networks. We were almost bragging about how easy it was for us to hire people. Now we are entering a different stage of the company where we need to get more experienced people in faster, and we can't find them fast enough using our networks.
>
> Fiona Nielsen, entrepreneur

Fiona has started to use recruiters to help identify and hire the specialists she needs to grow Repositive. She recognised that she and her colleagues had strong networks in the bioinformatics sphere but lacked other connections, such as the necessary commercial links. One of their recent searches using a recruiter was for a commercial director who had the specific skills and experience they needed to start opening channels into the biopharma sector.

Lord Bilimoria points out that it isn't always just about skills. Sometimes, the right people bring something else to the table.

> I think to hire the right people, the most important thing you're looking for is not their skills. You're looking for will as opposed to skill. Ideally both, but it's the attitude that counts, and if I see somebody has the right attitude, that's what counts in the end. I've got people like Samson Sohail, my head of sales, who's been by my side from the time I got married. People say I'm married to Samson as much as I'm married to my wife. Without his support over the years, without his loyalty, without his brilliance, I wouldn't be where I am today. So great, loyal team members with the right attitude make all the difference.
>
> Lord Bilimoria, entrepreneur

Team members will inevitably come from different backgrounds, and this can add to the complexity. Elin Haf Davies, who hadn't intended to set up a company at all, found herself doing something that she'd sworn she'd never do again: people management. She had plenty of experience from working in the NHS and felt that people management – or HR – didn't necessarily play to her strengths. She also found that the start-up world had complex HR issues of its own.

> Management, recruitment, payroll, HR is really time-consuming...As a start-up, you can set some objectives and targets today, and then something will happen tomorrow and you need to completely change. Some people are ok – [they] understand that it's a start-up and things change on a day-to-day basis. Other people, especially if they've spent the majority of their time in big corporates [aren't comfortable with] that rate of change. Having to balance 500 balls in the air at the same time is not everybody's cup of tea.
>
> Elin Haf Davies, entrepreneur

It's not just about putting the team together. You also have to think about the future. Are you putting together a team for the long-term, or just gathering a few of the skills you need for the next year or so? As with everything else, there are different schools of thought on this. Some entrepreneurs, and investors, believe that the team has to be refreshed regularly as the company grows, because different skillsets are needed at different stages. Others are firmly convinced that a strong team sticking together helps provide a solid foundation and consistent culture. Ramona Liberoff believes that a lot of the best start-up teams go the distance together, and founders should really think about how having a stable team could future-proof the business.

> They have a strong, trust-based relationship. They are not necessarily the same as each other, but they're able to stay as a roughly stable team and add what capacity they need on an

equal footing. They don't need to have known each other for long. What they need to uncover is whether they share the same values.

Ramona Liberoff, entrepreneur and investor

Carlos Diniz recognised that one of the reasons his dental clinic company eventually failed was that, because it was growing so fast, they couldn't hire the right people quickly enough to support the expansion.

We had sales of one million in the first year, two million in the second year, five million in the third year, seven in the fourth. We were running eleven million in the fifth year. With this amazing growth, you need people with track records in dealing with accelerated expansion. I realise some of them didn't have the experience of such a high growth rate. It was my fault: I chose them.

Carlos Diniz, entrepreneur

The problem was compounded by a lack of specialists to deliver the service in the dental clinics.

Whilst expanding, we couldn't find good people, so we had to split our teams to open new clinics. With that, plus internally not contracting new and good people, we had to go to a dental recruiter. In my opinion, in that specific market, that was a big mistake. We were contracting people through a recruiter who didn't know the sector, plus we were losing money and we were paying the recruiter. And yet we were the ones who knew about the business and the people we wanted, so that generated another problem in the company.

Carlos Diniz, entrepreneur

Getting the culture right
Another issue to consider when you start to grow the team is how it will impact on company culture. Start-ups necessarily have a

particular culture that isn't always comfortable, and the level of risk, hours of work and having to respond to rapid change can be too stressful for some.

> Recruiting the right talent who get the vision, have the right level of experience, and are comfortable with the dynamism and flux of a start-up is one of my top three challenges.
>
> Hakim Yadi, entrepreneur

Elin Haf Davies has seen how the nature of her business – applying tech to healthcare – has generated a particular culture, partly due to the fact that most of her tech team had never worked in healthcare while her healthcare team did not have a tech background. For both sides, the mission of the company chimes for different reasons.

> I do think they got excited and behind the bigger concept, having worked in things like financial tech services before. I think they are enjoying the opportunity to be in the field we're in now. And my other colleagues – they'd already worked in healthcare, so I think they're buying into the concept that we need innovation to start changing the clinical trials experience.
>
> Elin Haf Davies, entrepreneur

If you've managed to build a good core team from the start, that is where the culture starts to solidify. It's not necessarily something you create intentionally: if you're hiring people from very different backgrounds and with different skill sets, the culture will grow not only from the vision that they have signed up to, but also from the way the members of the team interact.

> We were lucky because we hired the right people without knowing much about how to hire people. It was just a personality fit. That is not to mean that we are all the same. We're actually very different.
>
> Gonçalo de Vasconcelos, entrepreneur

You can get lucky with your early hires, like Gonçalo, or you can take a few goes to get it right. Either way, those early hires will play a major role in developing the company culture.

> What I call the first wave of recruitment in SyndicateRoom was crucial in defining the culture of the company for the second wave of recruitment as we started scaling up. All of those people are still around. They are people that I trust entirely. They trust me entirely. We work really well as a team. It would have been impossible to get SyndicateRoom to where it is today without them.
>
> Gonçalo de Vasconcelos, entrepreneur

An important aspect of culture is attitude to failure. When everyone is intensely busy and many, if not all, of the team are new to entrepreneurial life, it can be tempting to try and cover up mistakes. But concealing errors not only creates internal tension in the person who makes them, it can also affect the chances of success for everybody. Founders have to admit to and learn from failures, and so do the rest of the team, and the only way to do this is to have an open and transparent culture that views mistakes as opportunities to learn rather than reasons to blame.

How culture can help in competing for talent – Toby's story

At the end of the day, it is all about the team. I have been told this so many times, but it seems to be a lesson that I relearn at least once a quarter in one way, shape, or form. Everyone gets that it's important to have high quality, motivated, ambitious people as part of your team. But how do you actually get that? How do you put that together?

Toby Norman, entrepreneur

We met Toby earlier. Simprints, the company he co-founded with three others, is focused on ways to deliver better healthcare in developing countries, to communities where medical records and the people they refer to are difficult to match up. A non-profit, the company is funded and partnered by organisations like the Bill and Melinda Gates Foundation, the UK Department for International Development, USAID, ARM, the Children's Investment Fund Foundation and Gavi (the vaccine alliance).

> *One of the challenges we have as a non-profit technology company is that we're competing for top technical talent with some of the biggest players in this space – players like Apple, Amazon. How do you compete on things like salaries against those players? So we've had to think very strategically. How do we actually get the best talent when those are the opportunities they're looking at?*

It became clear to Simprints early on that there was no point in competing for engineering talent with the likes of Amazon on the basis of salary alone. Since they were only able to offer considerably below what the giants could offer, they knew they would not recruit people who were focused on making money.

> *What we've learned is that you've got to think very strategically about your areas of relative strength. Don't waste time coming in 20, 30 or 50% below what Amazon can offer, because it's not going to seal the deal. Where you can compete, though, is in areas like purpose. Is there something meaningful to the work you're doing?*

What Simprints was able to offer was a sense of mission, a collective culture and a level of autonomy and freedom that the bigger corporates could not.

> *We think really hard about culture and team, and in these areas it's tough for Amazon to compete. No matter how exciting and huge the organisation is, at the end of the day it's not going to be making the type of difference to, for example, really poor children's lives in Bangladesh that an organisation like Simprints can make. So if we compete on those areas, we've got a much stronger change of landing the type of talent we need to solve the technical challenges we face.*

One of the ways Simprints demonstrates its confidence in the people the company hires is in the level of freedom, flexibility and responsibility employees have.

One thing Simprints does is unlimited paid time off. We screen very hard for people who are so passionate about making the world a better place and doing great engineering work that they're going to choose when they need to take a rest, refresh, and come back to work.

Toby Norman, entrepreneur

What do investors think?

When you're putting together your team, you're not just thinking about the skills balance and the passion for the vision. If you're going to need funding, then you should also keep in mind what potential investors will be looking for.

Bill T. Gross, founder of 'start-up studio' Idealab, strongly believed that the idea was key, closely linked to the personality and drive of the entrepreneur or founder. But he decided to test his belief by studying the 100-plus companies that had come through Idealab and an equal number of companies that had been funded and incubated elsewhere. He explained in a TED talk how he had tried to deconstruct the different elements that contributed to the most successful companies out of the 200 he analysed. Gross looked at what he considered to be the five most important factors for a start-up: the idea, the team, the business model, the funding and the timing. The aim was to demonstrate which of these factors was most important to a company's success or failure, and Gross was pretty convinced that the idea would come out on top. To his surprise, he found that timing and the team scored highest, at 42% and 32%, respectively. The idea came third, with a score of 28%.

Timing is a difficult attribute to assess. As Gross pointed out in his TED talk, the economic situation and availability of broadband were two key factors for several companies, some of which succeeded while others did not. The companies themselves weren't hugely different; it was just that they were founded at different times and under different external circumstances.

So it will come as no surprise that savvy investors look to pick winning teams. They will invest in a winning team with a good idea over a mediocre team with a brilliant idea because they understand the relative importance of these two elements. They also pick the teams that encompass the broadest range of skills, because they know that no one person has all the skills needed to get a company off the ground.

> When I talk to people who are thinking of starting a business, the one thing I say is that business is like a lottery where you need six numbers to win big. If you've got five numbers, you get ten quid, if you've got six numbers, you get ten million. I've never met an entrepreneur that's had more than four. I think I have three. I think Charles Dunstone has four. Somebody else has got the other numbers, and you've got to find them to make up your team.
>
> Neil McArthur, entrepreneur and investor

For Jon Bradford, the team is also first – but it's the market that comes next.

> There are only two things that matter in my head. One is the people, and two is how big is the market. We had this simple rule, which was if we knew nothing about the background of the business – what they did, the product, whether they are an investment – and the only decision you could make was the people standing in front of you, did you believe the story and would you invest in them on a personal level?
>
> Jon Bradford, entrepreneur and investor

But Jon qualifies that with a few words of caution: 'Never fall in love with the idea of the product. Never fall in love with the co-founders, or the co-investors.' Many investors understand that emotion can all too easily cloud judgement. So create the best team you possibly can if you're looking for investment, but don't rely on strength of personality to sway the funders. Make sure to have all the facts and figures covered.

Moving people on: the difficult decision to fire

> One of the key things is not being afraid to move people on.
>
> Luke Hakes, investor

The nature of the start-up journey means that, sooner or later, team members will leave. They may leave of their own accord, perhaps because they don't feel they fit the culture after all, or they no longer feel motivated by the idea behind the business, or they have had a better offer and their loyalty isn't strong.

> It's a high-performance culture. That's not to mean that it's long hours. It's just working really smartly and having fun. That's crucial, because we all spend so much time in the office. Most of our waking hours are in the office. You have to enjoy it. You have to really love what you're doing and the people you're working with. If you're not, you're better off going elsewhere, to be honest. And that's really important for us – that we have communal tables for people to sit around with their laptops like a café…even if they're working on different things. That's really important. People have left and they were mostly people that didn't really fit into that culture.
>
> Gonçalo de Vasconcelos, entrepreneur

At other times, however, you will need to ask people to leave, and that is a hard decision to make, especially when there are only a few of you and any departure will have a big impact. Luke Hakes has a good analogy for the situation.

> If you think of a start-up as a boat, there's only enough space, probably, for five or six, and they all have to row hard. If you've got someone who's not rowing, you need them out, even if they're a founding member of the team. That is a really tough decision for CEOs and founders, and actually for investors.
>
> Luke Hakes, investor

Although it might seem from their earlier comments that Gonçalo and Tom, co-founders of SyndicateRoom, have had it easy when hiring people – their first hire, Fran, for example, has grown with the company from the very early days – things haven't always gone quite as well.

> One of the things we needed to learn was to fire fast. Both Tom and I are too nice sometimes, which works great for some things but not for others. Sometimes, you have this sneaking suspicion about someone and you need to act on it.
>
> Gonçalo de Vasconcelos, entrepreneur

'Hire slow and fire fast', as the saying goes. You do have to be tough because, like Luke's analogy, the boat won't go anywhere if someone is rowing in the wrong direction.

Lord Bilimoria acknowledges that sometimes problems are caused when the wrong hiring decisions are made – and it's not necessarily the employee's fault.

> When you hire the wrong people, they can almost destroy your business. I've made the mistake of hiring the wrong people and you can't blame them. You have to take the blame because you hired them.
>
> Lord Bilimoria, entrepreneur

There may also come a time when you have to fire someone because they are no longer right for the business. A start-up might change so rapidly that some employees lag behind in terms of the skills needed, and you have to take the right decision for the business, however hard that feels.

> It's about having the right people in the right seats at the right time. There's no point in hiring somebody going, "Oh, in five years' time we're going to be 10,000 people. I need a sales manager that's going to be able to manage that many people." You only hire for the next 12 to 18 months, and if that person is

not going to work out 18 months after that, change the person. Everybody is on a short life cycle until they can prove that they can scale with the company. It's not like you've got a steady business. The business is scaling and the people need to scale with the company, and that's hard to assess in advance.

Luke Hakes, investor

And then there are the times when circumstances dictate that you have to shrink your workforce, typically when revenues and funding are squeezed, or the business pivots and a new skills mix is needed. Ronjon Nag had the difficult task of taking his company down from 70 people to 7 when they were between funding rounds, while Fiona Nielsen and her management team realised that the skills mix was wrong if they were to meet their next targets. But as she describes, redundancies handled well can end up as a positive experience.

Our next stage of company milestones was all about delivering product to market, and the composition of our team had to be refocused. It didn't make sense for the company to have big expenses in, for example, marketing and outreach until we had the product ready to market. So we did a restructuring where we had to make some redundancies and had to let people go because they weren't what the company needed at the time.

It was really difficult because you felt like you were saying goodbye to a family member, and we learned how you have to distinguish between your personal relationship and what the company needs. As it turns out, once the people who were affected by the restructuring understood the reasoning behind it, they took it very well and were very supportive of the change, realising that it was what Repositive needed, and they wanted the company to succeed. I've been in touch with all of them recently and they've all gone on to find new jobs, so change is not necessarily bad, it's just change. Morale has fully recovered, both in the people who left and the people who stayed.

Fiona Nielsen, entrepreneur

THREE THINGS ABOUT BUILDING THE CORE TEAM

- Most entrepreneurs say building the core team is difficult, so don't be surprised if you find it challenging to understand what you need and where to find the right people.
- The team must represent the skills mix the business needs now and in the short-term. Don't hire for what you think the business will look like in five years' time: you have to have the skills to get there first.
- 'Hire slow, fire fast' is a good policy to adopt.

CHAPTER 5

Investors

> **I'm always surprised at how little entrepreneurs understand about investors and how they make their decisions.**

The entrepreneurs that we surveyed all included raising money as one of their top three challenges. Few businesses scale rapidly on customer revenue alone, so inevitably you will have to find some funding from somewhere along the way. However, it can be difficult to decide what type of investment and which investor(s) are right for your company. This chapter looks at the big picture of funding and investors, but there's a lot more detail on the practical aspects of funding in our first book, *The Invested Investor*.

There are many different sources of funding for start-ups and growing companies, from friends and family to venture capital (VC) firms, and from bank loans to government grants. There are incubators, accelerators, start-up labs and groups of angels all looking for the next star entrepreneurs.

Each source of funding has its advantages and disadvantages. Grants and loans may sound like a good deal as you won't have to give up any equity in your business in exchange, but they can be heavy on the paperwork and rigid in the application of terms and conditions. Loans also need some form of security, which you may not have or may not wish to risk losing.

Other forms of investment – principally angel or VC funding – mean giving up a share of your business. You and your co-founders, if there are any, will no longer be the outright owners of 100% of the company you set up. Many founders are not comfortable with the loss of control that shared ownership can bring. Others set a limit that feels right to them: too small a share in the company you founded may make you wonder why you even work there.

Choosing the wrong investors could scupper your business at some point, perhaps because they fail to follow on or insist on a trade sale so they can get their money back before you feel you've really hit your stride. Some founders discover the hard way that their charming investors are not so benevolent after all and end up with little to show for all their hard work.

Understanding what type of investment is right for you takes time and effort, but it is worth putting in the work as good investors bring much more to your business than just money. They can help you in all sorts of ways, many of which you might not even have thought of yet. Their sector expertise and advice could help your company grow, find customers, meet key people and support you towards the next round of funding.

> Investors come in different shapes and sizes. Some investors are really focused on the team and the founders. Some are interested in innovative business models. Some just like really novel products. Some like exploring new markets. So it really,

really depends on where your unique selling point lies. What is your strength? What differentiates you from the crowd of other start-ups trying to raise funds?

Jessica Dick, entrepreneur and investor

The message is to do as much due diligence on your investors as they will be doing on you. Yes, it takes time when you'd rather be focusing on growing your business, but that time should be repaid through the benefits that the right investors can bring.

When should you raise money?

I've met a lot of entrepreneurs who consider investment way too late.

Jessica Dick, entrepreneur and investor

The answer to the question of when to raise money is, 'before you need it', or even, 'before you know you need it'. Running out of cash is a frequent reason for business failure, and while you've been putting all your effort into perfecting your business plan, you also need to develop a funding plan alongside it.

If you don't plan your investment strategy, you will find yourself scrambling for investment when things are getting tight, and may well end up getting funding from the wrong type of investors simply because you're desperate for anything you can get.

The hardest thing is when you're rushed: when you're running out of cash and you need to get investors quickly. It's very likely that you're going to choose the wrong investor or the wrong deal, or even potentially miss some key information and not be aligned with the investors, just because you haven't had the time to build the best case for your investment.

Jessica Dick, entrepreneur and investor

But many entrepreneurs fall into that trap because they do not realise how long it takes to raise money. It is crucial to do your sums so you know how much investment you need to keep operating until the next round closes.

> It can take a good six months to raise an investment. That's an average, not the longest time it can take. Make sure you have that sort of runway so that you can raise the investment in the best way for your company.
>
> Jessica Dick, entrepreneur and investor

Emily Mackay found that once the first investor came on board, securing the rest of the round was easier. But getting that first investor took up a lot of her time.

> As CEO, I spend arguably way too much of my time chasing finance, trying to get extra funding. Earlier rounds got stretched out and we ended up with multiple closures. The first closure was the hardest. When you have a follow-on period, a whole bunch of people come in because it's de-risked. They can see that people have definitely closed, signed the paperwork and transferred the money, and it gives them a lot of reassurance.
>
> Emily Mackay, entrepreneur

Similarly, Ofri Ben-Porat was also surprised at the amount of time he needed to put into raising funds. A big problem was that he was not only trying to raise money, but also to generate and close sales at the same time; the business nearly collapsed because he simply didn't have enough hours in the day to do both. The company hired its first Chief Commercial Officer, who quickly diagnosed the problem. Sales conversations have to be initiated and then take time to bring to close. Studying Ofri's schedule revealed several months where no new conversations were initiated, and negotiations already under way stalled while Ofri was focusing on investors.

> I think that's my first learning from doing a round. It's either you go in full-time, or you don't do it. It gets easier as you go

on, because you hire the CCO, or a Head of Commercial, so next time, there's somebody to keep the company going while you're doing the round.

Ofri Ben-Porat, entrepreneur

How much should you raise?

It's been a good discipline to raise relatively small rounds. But at the same time, it's never really enabled us to build a team.

Adam Kerr, entrepreneur

If you don't raise enough in one round, you'll find yourself tied up in another fund-raising round before you've consolidated any gains from the previous round. Be ambitious, because you'll always need more than you expect, but not so ambitious that you put people off.

One of the biggest fails I see is people saying, "We just need 150,000 to get this done and then we'll raise more," or, "We just need another 300,000 on top," where, in fact, if you had another million, two million, three million…you could destroy your competition. I think people are afraid to raise big because they're afraid of the answer.

Ofri Ben-Porat, entrepreneur

It can be hard for very early-stage businesses to raise big sums, but if you're thinking long-term and have great ambitions, looking for small chunks of investment will hold you back and may prevent you from reaching your goals altogether.

If I ask, "How much do you need to beat your competition?" and they say, "Four million would be really good," then why not ask for four million? I think VCs nowadays ask, "What's the drive for this company? How big is the vision if they're only asking for two million? Come ask for six, we'll give you six."

Ofri Ben-Porat, entrepreneur

However, some believe that too much too soon can be as damaging as not raising enough. If VC investors with deep pockets had injected $100 million into chip designer ARM in the early days, the company might have changed its business model and tried to become a chip maker big enough to challenge the giants Intel and AMD. Being forced to keep as lean as possible and focus on designing fast, efficient, low-power processors, ARM was able to leverage its unique capabilities and grow into a company worth more than $30 billion.

> [US companies Etagen and Achates] raised their first $100 million in less time that it took us to raise the first $5 million…[This] forces an ascetic mindset that can be a source of competitive advantage, since it helps us focus on the most valuable activities and model.
>
> Sam Cockerill, entrepreneur

The amount you raise has to be based on sensible calculations around how much you need to keep paying salaries and developing your product until the next round of funding, with sufficient extra to tide you over if that round comes in later than expected. But the amount also has to be tied to your vision. How much will make that vision come true? In the end, it's a balancing act between too little and too much, and getting the amount just right is as much an art as a science.

Where might your funding come from?
The most typical sources of funds for start-ups and growing companies are business angels and VCs. Our previous book, *The Invested Investor*, tells you all you need to know about the way the most committed business angels think and invest. It's worth taking the time to understand their motives and perspectives, as they're the people you'll need to persuade to back your company.

In between – or sometimes alongside – angels and VCs, there is a middle ground of grants and project funding from public or other institutions specifically intended to help start-ups. Some grants are tied to product development, others to commercial development, and many start-ups find them an invaluable way to prove their concept or produce a minimum viable product which will help them to secure the next stage of funding. For instance, grants from the UK's Technology Strategy Board (now Innovate UK) helped SwiftKey develop a prototype of its predictive typing app and subsequently secure over $20 million in VC funding. SwiftKey was acquired by Microsoft for $250 million in 2016, six years after it launched its first app.

Innovate UK has supported around 11,000 projects in 8,000 organisations over the past decade, leading to as much as a £16 billion increase in gross value added to the economy. Innovate UK helps businesses through making connections and providing funding at all stages, from pre-start-ups and SMEs to the largest PLCs.

> Smaller businesses often come direct to us with a specific proposal for grant funding to carry out a particular research and development project. That can work very well alongside angel investment or early stage VC investment, or the founder's own funds.
>
> Nigel Walker, head of innovation

Grant funding may be associated with a defined area or sector and open to competition. The money is intended to reimburse some of the project costs and effectively de-risks it, enabling the company to do something that it might otherwise not have been able to do. For instance, Innovate UK may fund up to 70% of costs for a feasibility study, or around 60% for proof of concept or industrial research. Developing a prototype may also be supported by a grant or particularly by innovation loans, which are aimed at micro, small or medium-sized businesses, i.e. those with up to 250 employees.

> Businesses need to demonstrate that they have a really good idea, that there's a really good market, that they can deliver a project, that they need public sector funding support and that they're not just doing it for fun.
>
> Nigel Walker, head of innovation

Grant funding bodies thus have a different perspective to angel and other forms of investment. The latter look at the company as a whole rather than just one particular element. However, they often work alongside each other, with a start-up perhaps seeking grant-funding for product development and angel funding to build the company.

> The two activities are very complementary. Whilst an angel investor may be thinking that they want to see a company succeed, they want to see some value creation that leads to a successful exit…Our perspective, on behalf of the taxpayer, is to look at it and see: how does the economy grow? Are jobs created? Is industry transformed so that it's fit for the future?
>
> Nigel Walker, head of innovation

Whatever the benefits – such as keeping ownership or accessing unattached funds to enable you to reach proof of concept – there are drawbacks to grant funding, and one of these is that grants are rarely big enough to get you the whole way. Sooner or later, you will need to look for money elsewhere.

Another source of early-stage funding is the accelerator. Y Combinator, which was founded in 2005, has seen some spectacular successes. Based in Silicon Valley, Y Combinator selects a few companies each year to receive funding and mentorship, along with the networking opportunities that being part of such an organisation can bring. In return, it takes a single-figure equity stake in each business. Among the household names Y Combinator has helped produce are Dropbox, Airbnb and Reddit. According to its website, more than 2,000 start-ups have received funding from Y Combinator, and the combined valuation of those that survived is over $100 billion.

UK innovation forum Nesta found that there were 163 accelerators and 11 pre-accelerators in the UK in 2017, along with 7 virtual accelerators and 205 incubators. Calculations suggested these organisations were investing around £33 million each year in start-ups. But with nearly half the accelerators based in London, provisions are not evenly spread around the country.

Accelerators have specific criteria for the companies they engage with, and you need to ensure that meeting those criteria does not mean disrupting your business model or changing your idea just to have a chance of getting accelerator funding. You have to consider carefully whether the programme is right for you and your company.

 You shouldn't build a business to be on an accelerator.

Jon Bradford, entrepreneur and investor

Corporate venturing can be very different from other types of venture capital. These funds tend to look for companies and technologies that are in the investor company's sector, potentially disrupters, potentially an acquisition when they are more mature. For instance, British Gas came in on an investment round for AlertMe, which led to an eventual acquisition as AlertMe's product was incorporated into the British Gas Hive smart home system.

Being creative about sources of funding – Lord Bilimoria's story

When Karan Bilimoria and Arjun Reddy co-founded Cobra Beer in 1989, they had £20,000 of student debt to pay off and no spare cash, so they had to raise all of the money they needed.

Bilimoria recognised that their most valuable asset was going to be their brand, and if they built value in the business and the brand, then the shares the co-founders held would grow in value – hence he was keen to maintain as much ownership as he could without having to give some up to investors. But having no assets, no collateral and no security meant that raising money was going to be tricky. They started with an unsecured bank overdraft of £7,500, and then a larger overdraft from another bank.

I realised very quickly that to have good advisors can help you raise money. So we worked with Grant Thornton very early on, and they helped us...When a proposal and a business plan came from Grant Thornton, it added credibility [so] people would at least listen to us and give us a chance. We'd still get lots of "noes", but at least we got a chance to try... Grant Thornton helped us raise our first angel investment – £50,000 for five percent of our business, valuing it at a million pounds.

Lord Bilimoria, entrepreneur

Interest rates were up at 15% when Bilimoria and Reddy started Cobra, so they had to be very innovative about how and where they raised money. For them, with fast-growing sales associated with a fast-growing brand but no security in the form of bricks and mortar or other assets, getting enough working capital to keep pace with the growth was key. And as Lord Bilimoria describes it, the funding strategy had to grow to keep up with the needs of the company.

We went for everything we could get. We had loans under the government small firms loan guarantee scheme totalling £250,000...that really helped us get Cobra off the ground. We had unsecured loans – the owner of the brewery in India would get his friends to invest in us on his word, all down to trust.

Then we raised money with Grant Thornton's help through cumulative, redeemable preference shares...Different forms of trade finance...Bills of exchange – where one of our biggest customers in the UK blocked off a chunk of their overdraft facility, and when a container was delivered from India, they would sign a bill of exchange, we'd get their bankers to endorse it and take it to our bank, so we had money guaranteed by Barclays, which was like cash.

We very quickly learned, for a growing business like ours, [that] we could raise finance from growing sales, so we started factoring. When you factor, you get 75 percent of your sales the day you make them. Then we graduated to invoice discounting – when you're factoring, your customers know you're doing it. When you're invoice discounting, it's confidential, and it's much cheaper as well. Then we graduated to invoice financing, and that was a great way of financing...At one stage, we were getting 90% of our money on the day we made the sale or the next day.

Lord Bilimoria, entrepreneur

From an accelerator to a VC – Ofri's story

Ofri Ben-Porat founded his company Pixoneye – now known as Edgify – in Tel Aviv, but went to Web Summit in Dublin in search of funding. A week later, he found himself pitching for funding from marketing and advertising tech accelerator Collider.

> We went to Dublin with a terrible-looking Power Point presentation on loop. We went there with zero expectations…A lady walked by; she seemed fairly interested, but not too interested. She said, "Give it to me in ten seconds," so I did what I could. She said, "That's actually a bit more interesting," and gave me a bit more time…Later, she said, "We're closing our first fund round for 2015, why don't you come and speak to the board next week?"
>
> Ofri Ben-Porat, entrepreneur

Ofri flew to London and gave his pitch to the board and investors of Collider. The model for Collider was to award £50,000 to ten companies and then, four months later, an additional £100,000 for the top five of those ten companies. Ofri secured the £50,000, and then his company came out top four months later and received the additional funds.

The funding from Collider was the team's first investment, and today they call it the 'friends and family round' because the people at Collider have become close friends and associates.

> The great thing about Collider is that it's a network of angels that invest under one hat. We deal with one person in shareholder meetings [but] we have 18 ex-CMOs, ex-CEOs, ex-founders who have all come in, and because they have all invested very little, they are not high-level investors who are disconnected from reality and what's going on in business. They still have contacts in their industries.

The funding from Collider came not only with mentoring and advice from those who had invested directly, but also gave Ofri plenty of other opportunities.

> We didn't know anything about London and the UK. Collider had events, so I kept coming back and forth from Israel to London to meet the

investors, to attend the events, meet potential clients. What it did was set us up for the next funding round.

Four months after the £100,000 from Collider, Ofri raised a further £400,000. As he says, they had a good team of engineers and researchers in place, but the £150,000 in total from Collider 'went by in an instant'. For this next round, some of the Collider investors continued, but Ofri knew they needed to look further afield to make up the total as the company was still two years away from getting a product into the market. For him, the networking effect of being part of Collider came up with the goods.

> *Off the back of Collider, I met somebody who sits on the committee of the Harvard Business School Angel Association. He pushed me to go to their committee. They pass four companies a quarter to their network and you do a 20-minute pitch.*

Ofri wasn't sure it was worth the investment of flying to the US for a 20-minute pitch but entered his plan anyway, and when he was told that they had made it to the final pitch, the decision was made. The event featured not only the committee, but also members of the HBS Angel Association.

> *I was told to come with term sheets ready, printed, because these guys come with cheque books. I thought that was a joke, so I didn't go with term sheets. I finished my pitch. You're supposed to go outside and wait until everybody finishes…As I'm going out, this guy follows me and says, "Listen, I've got to run but I'm in for 50,000, where do I sign?" And I said, "What do you mean you're in for 50,000? You don't know the terms." He says, "Love it, I'm in for 50,000." So I took a piece of paper and I wrote 50,000, I wrote his name down.*

> Ofri Ben-Porat, entrepreneur

Having been vetted by the committee was enough for several more investors at the event, and over the next few days, Ofri raised £250,000 from about 10 angels. A Russian investment fund also came in, and the funding was Ofri's signal to move to London for the next stage of the business.

Getting investment ready

If you're going to secure funding from angel or VC investors, you need to demonstrate a number of things to convince them that you and your business deserve their money and will generate a return for them.

> There are five things that you should have in place before you go out to raise investment. You might not have all five, but if you have a good combination of three of them, you can then race around to achieve the other two.
>
> Jessica Dick, entrepreneur and investor

Jessica's five requirements are: a minimum viable product (MVP), a credible team, a viable business model, early signs of product–market fit and a strong plan for growth. Other investors will have their own criteria and, if they have websites, these will usually be listed. There's nothing worse than approaching an investor who has no interest in your sector or taking the the wrong pack of information, so make sure to check.

> At the start-up stage, the principle thing we look for is domain expertise. Does this individual understand the market they're going after? Do they understand the nuances in that market? Are they solving a problem that exists and that people think is valuable?
>
> Luke Hakes, investor

You also have to make sure everything is in place and clearly documented and explained, as you may not get to meet potential investors until fairly late in the process. Although we often hear about founder/investor relationships starting at networking or pitching events, some investors are more cautious. They don't want to be swayed by the personalities of the core team, and instead focus on the business and the strategy. This is their way of avoiding 'falling in love' with the people rather than making a rational decision based on the business.

> Many founders are exceptionally charismatic individuals. And human beings are fallible. We are emotional. We respond socially rather than intellectually...so we took away the personal pitch until the very end of the process, whereas before, it had started with it. And our predictions of success actually went way up. In a perfect case, the charisma goes alongside the integrity, but not always.
>
> Ramona Liberoff, entrepreneur and investor

Finding out your company isn't structured for investment – Emily's story

When you set up a company, it has to have a legal structure. There are options, but be careful, because how you set your company up can affect your chances of finding investment. Emily Mackay discovered this when she set up her first company, Microgenius. The company was founded with very good intentions to help the renewable energy market, and Emily thought she was doing the right thing in choosing a slightly unusual corporate model.

> At the time, what I was trying to do was something that bordered on a non-profit – which isn't actually a legal structure, more of a principle that can be enshrined in a legal structure...I chose a non-traditional legal structure, so not a company limited by shares. Not a co-operative, but a company limited by guarantee, which isn't that well known, but basically means you don't have shares in the company, which at the time seemed to accord with the social principles I was trying to generate. We weren't going to be doing this for profit, we were going to be doing this for the good of the need for renewable energy.
>
> Emily Mackay, entrepreneur

The problem for Emily was that she had created something which had no vehicle for funders to invest in. She remembers some 'very blank angels' faces' because they couldn't see a way to invest, and they wondered why she was pitching to them at all. Eventually, she sat down with one angel and went through the problem and worked out how to wrap an investible structure around the company but, as she says, now she would do things differently.

It propelled me onto bigger things, so actually it was sort of a happy mistake because it forced me to accelerate some of the activity. I couldn't go out and raise lots of capital, so I had to make do with very small amounts and prove things very, very quickly. So, constraint of capital wasn't necessarily a bad thing.

For Emily's second company, Crowd Surfer (later rebranded as TAB), she learned from her earlier mistakes and had a great deal more success in raising funding.

I raised three or four rounds, but we had multiple closures in each round, so I think we had six closures in total over the life of what became TAB because this was a company with shares, a normal company structure. Each round we incremented on valuation and we incremented on amount as well.

Emily Mackay, entrepreneur

Choose your investors wisely

❝ Don't raise money just for the money.

Carlos Diniz, entrepreneur

Different kinds of cash come with different headaches, different benefits and different drawbacks. Cash is not a commodity but part of a bigger picture, and finding the right investors can bring you cash with benefits.

❝ I've seen what a good board or set of investors can do for a company, and I've seen what a disengaged investor, or not having investors at all, can do. The benefit of having a really active, supportive investor base can do wonders for a company.

Jessica Dick, entrepreneur and investor

Several entrepreneurs have told us about the importance of doing due diligence on investors – just as they're doing due diligence on the founders and the company – because having the wrong investors on board can cause its own kind of problems.

> The biggest lesson I learnt is investors are very capable and wise and they really know a lot about markets, but people looking for investment should find investors with track records in things they need. If they want to take a product to market, they should find investors who have a track record in going to market. If they want to recruit a lot of people, they should find investors with that experience. Track records are everything when you are a start-up, because a small failure can kill you.
>
> Jessica Dick, entrepreneur and investor

What sort of investors do you need? As usual, that depends. Do you have in-depth knowledge of the sector you're going into? If so, then look for investors with experiences and skills that will add to, not duplicate, yours. Do you have very little knowledge of the sector you're going into? Then find investors who have the understanding you need.

> It's all about complementarity. If a founder has solid foundations in their company's sector themselves, it could be quite interesting for them to have a perspective from another sector, because there are always lessons that can be learned. I think that's when some very exciting things have happened in the start-up space, when you see stuff that's been applied for years in a certain industry applied to another.
>
> But if the founders are launching in an industry that they really don't understand or don't know, then it's absolutely crucial for them to get [sector knowledge] as part of the mix.
>
> Jessica Dick, entrepreneur and investor

You also need to pay attention to timing. Whereas grants are typically for a time-limited project, other investments may also come with different timescales attached. Angels could have enough in their investment pot to stick with you for all of the early years and several funding rounds, but that is unusual, and at some point, they will stop following on.

> These days there is a lot more choice of VC. Do the home-work, do the due diligence on the VC and don't be lazy. Call the portfolio companies to understand how the VC operates, what they actually bring to the deals, what sort of personalities they are – because there are very different management styles, too.
>
> Max Bautin, investor

VCs are in a different position to angels because they are managing other people's money invested into funds that usually have a time limit to them (so-called 'patient' VCs are the exception to this, and take a much longer-term perspective). So an important question to ask when looking for VC funding is how old the fund is and how long it has to go – if a VC fund invests a year or two before the end of a fund, the pressure to produce a return quickly will be dispro-portionate and there probably won't be any follow-on funding. You would expect VCs not to do this because the risks are so high, but if other companies in that investment portfolio have already failed, or do not need additional funding, they might be looking for some-where to put their extra money in the hope of a fast return.

> A VC that invests in the first year of a fund and a VC that invests in the fifth year of their fund will be on a different time expectation…Ability to follow on is what matters.
>
> Max Bautin, investor

Then there's the question of how many investors you need. The answer will depend on your situation. Do you need several inves-tors who bring a range of skills and contacts to the table, or only one or two to fill in the gaps? If you have a lot of investors, how will you manage them?

❝ I think any more than three VCs, you're already starting to be
in a situation where herding the cats is quite tough. Because,
inevitably, VCs have different maturities of funds, different fund sizes, a different approach to investments, different
personalities.

Max Bautin, investor

One VC may be easier to manage, but may not bring enough useful
contacts and experience to the table. Two VCs could result in a
good balance, if they work together well, and generally by Series B,
two or more VCs is much more common. The company will be at
a different stage in its growth and will need not only more investment, but also broader networks and wider connections, which an
additional VC can provide.

However, the problems are compounded when you reach the
stage of VC investment because there is so much more complexity.
You need your investors to be able to work together, which can be
a challenge because of the differences between them. You might
find that the time spent securing investment is equalled by the time
spent responding to your investors' particular requirements.

❝ We had three completely different investors in our early round.
We'd raised a couple of million, and they each had a similar
share. None of them wanted the same things, so you'd spend
ten days preparing a board pack for three completely different
sets of investors – complete waste of time and a real drag on a
small business that had enough complexity.

The difference was in investment hypothesis. Two were
impact investors who were interested in the social impact
that we were making…However, they had different metrics
to measure that social impact, so the measurement frame-
works that we had to use were unbelievably complex. The
others were mainstream VCs who had a good track record in
selling on IP, which is exactly what happened in this case. So
the investors at some point got together, did a deal amongst
themselves, and that's what enabled the team to be dismissed

and the profit accrue to the investors rather than to any of the people that actually created the business.

Ramona Liberoff, entrepreneur and investor

Is equity the be-all and end-all?

Securing funding generally means giving up some equity in your company. Naturally, investors want something that they hope will grow and be worth more over time so that they can get a return on their investment. Of course, we know that, in many cases, that return won't materialise, but it's still the driving force behind any investment.

You may also need to use shares, or share options, as part of remuneration packages to attract particular members of staff, so you have to decide how much you're willing to give up.

There are no guidelines for deciding how much equity you should keep, and sometimes you'll be in a position where you don't have much of an option. Ofri Ben-Porat has a potentially contro-versial opinion.

> I think you run a company on capital, not on shares. I can hire employees with capital; I can't do it with shares. I can build new tech, we can rent offices with capital. I've seen a lot of people…negotiating their hearts out for that extra 1%, extra 2%. I don't have much equity in the company, but I have a really big dream to sell it for north of a billion…You real-ise over time that, a) you need the capital, and b) if you have taken on the right people, the equity is worth so much more… and it's not worth losing sleep over. And I did lose a lot of sleep over it in the beginning.
>
> Ofri Ben-Porat, entrepreneur

When shareholders aren't right for the business

> The one thing that you cannot change about your company is your shareholders – especially if they are VCs – so you have to be very disciplined in terms of understanding what kind

of investor you are bringing in and what they will actually do for the company. Most VCs say they will do a lot, and a lot of them are not actually able to do quite as much as they say they can.

Max Bautin, investor

You can't fire a shareholder like you can fire an employee. They own part of the company and they have a right to stick around. But sometimes you might feel that they are not helping the business to grow. You might even feel that they are toxic to the business – for instance, if they are constantly challenging your decisions and wanting frequent updates in minute detail. In that situation, they could be taking up too much of your time: time that could be more productively spent growing the business.

What can you do? Very little. It's not even like a marriage, where divorce is an option. However, if you have enough support from co-founders and other board members, enough time and a good legal system around you, it might be possible to buy an investor out. But this is a serious decision to make, and could have all sorts of consequences, not least in terms of your time and team morale during what could be a lengthy and controversial process.

An alternative solution is to change the relationship. Find a way to reduce the troublesome investor's impact on you and the company, whether that be through finding an intermediary to manage the relationship, or by removing them from a board position. However you do it, you cannot afford to have one of your investors ruining things for everyone else.

Taking the wrong money – Carlos' story

Carlos Diniz founded his chain of dental clinics during a recession in Portugal, when premises were cheap and unemployment was high (making wage costs lower). He spotted the opportunity to open clinics in shopping centres, and launched his second clinic only a few months after the first. Yet, while he had proved the model and saw plenty of opportunity to expand, he couldn't get funding from the banks. The recession and financial crisis in Portugal had made the banks highly risk-averse. So in the end, Carlos had to go to private investors. After a lot of pitches, he was luckily in a position to choose the investors he felt were the best ones to share his journey, and a phase of rapid expansion began.

> *The most important thing to choose is the fit – not the money. I had better financial proposals, but I didn't have the fit with those investors. I could have had more money at the beginning…but I really and truly believe that people make all the difference. I really needed the support of those guys. I really wanted the money, too, but I wanted smart money. Even today, I think I made the best choice.*
>
> Carlos Diniz, entrepreneur

With this new investment, Carlos' dental chain grew rapidly to 12 clinics.

> *By 2013, we had opened clinic after clinic, we had no debt, we had double digit growth, we were like money printing machines. Things were very good, things were great. And then suddenly we had a proposal for a new investor to enter the company.*

The proposal was for a game-changing investment. It would mean Carlos losing his majority ownership of the company, but he was offered a 'golden stake' that would keep him as CEO and make him very rich indeed over the next few years. He was already planning another big expansion, along with moving into Spain – a market five times larger than that of Portugal – and so this was a very interesting offer. Nevertheless, he told the new investor that he would test the proposition in Spain and talk later again in the year.

But, as he admits, at this point he already knew that things were starting to go wrong. The company was at an inflection point, with a dozen clinics already open and ambitious plans to expand, and Portugal was beginning to come out of recession.

> *Portugal was now leaving the crisis and banks approached us and said…"We want to give you money, you are a very good company." So we accepted it. It was a mistake, we should not have accepted so much*

money. From that point forward, we did a lot of very good things, but also a lot of things that we shouldn't have done.

Carlos Diniz, entrepreneur

The company began to build new clinics and buy more expensive medical equipment to put in them. But they became overstretched and couldn't hire enough high-calibre staff to provide the dental services they wanted to offer. They had 12 clinics when they accepted the money; by the time the company went bankrupt, that number was up to 22.

Keeping investors on-side – Dominic's story

The investors had steam coming out of their ears.

Dominic Hill, entrepreneur

Dominic Hill faced a struggle when he realised that his original business model – the one his funders had invested in – wasn't going to work. He could see a way to a new model that he was convinced would succeed, but his investors were still sold on the original idea and, despite the problems they could see, wanted him to stick to the first plan. Not only that, but one of his co-founders was having serious doubts.

> *I remember one pivotal board meeting in Clerkenwell when I had raging fires all around me. We were burning cash. We were running out of runway. The investors had steam coming out of their ears. And one of my co-founders had just exploded in the kitchen and couldn't take the heat. He had made promises to his family and promises to us that were good as long as the [product] build didn't last longer than 18 months. And when it did, suddenly he had to choose his family over us, so he abandoned us mid-build. It was an absolute nightmare scenario.*

Essentially, Dominic was proposing a pivot, which would need more money and time – neither of which he had. However, he was so convinced he was right that he knew he had to find a way around all the misgivings.

I remember walking into that board meeting and saying, "I know it's not ideal timing, but I've got this idea I want to talk to you about.". . . I didn't get approval from the board in that meeting, but I did it anyway, because – as investors know – a true entrepreneur. . . will somehow have the courage to follow through on their gut instinct. So I put one engineer on it quietly. And we only had two engineers, so that was half my resource. It was massive at the time, and then we got a minimum viable product together and I quietly started getting traction on it.

We delivered huge amounts of software on a shoestring budget. To this day, one of my investors says he's never seen a team deliver as much software. He can't believe what we delivered on the money that went into the company.

Ultimately, I got to the position with our board where we were all convinced that this new model was right, but it happened over a series of very difficult meetings, one after the other after the other, where I really had a challenge on my hands every time. I wasn't sleeping before. I was having night sweats. It was really, really tough.

Dominic Hill, entrepreneur

It took 14 months of hard work – and even harder board meetings – until Dominic could switch off the eCommerce personalised website that his company was running and focus the business entirely on the platform he envisioned: an enterprise jewellery network connecting manufacturers, wholesalers, brands and retailers.

THREE THINGS ABOUT INVESTORS

- Don't just sit back while potential investors do due diligence on you and your company. Do your own due diligence on them to make sure they're right for the business.
- Different investors have different criteria for investing; make sure you fit their profile.
- Try not to be in a position where you have to take whatever is offered; an investment in your company should be about more than just money.

The board, advisors and mentors

> In this space, people love to share. That's why investors invest. They share their network, they open up their experience and their skills, but you need to know what you want and what you need help with.

You will need help. Even a serial entrepreneur can face new challenges, and having the right group of supporters in place – whether they are on the board, part of a separate advisory board, or your personal mentor – could be the difference between success and failure.

So board members, advisors and mentors are an important part of the team you create to help grow your company. They will usually bring skills and experience that you cannot buy in, and, if you bring the right group together, will help enormously with the ups and downs of your entrepreneurial journey.

But what's the difference between a board member, an advisor and a mentor? Sometimes nothing, sometimes the distinction will be clear if you have both a governance board and an advisory board. A mentor may also be an investor – one who has a vested interest in making sure you do your best with their money – but they may not necessarily sit on the board. Equally, a board member may be an investor – and this is particularly the case when you have investment from a group of angels or a VC: they will want to nominate a board member to keep an eye on how their funds are spent.

As your company grows, your board will evolve and the people on it may change. So it is important to remember that the board is there to serve the company, and when a board member is no longer right for the company, they should step down so that the right person can be brought in. Advisors and mentors, too, may fade away when their contributions are no longer required, although some will be there for the long haul.

The importance of good governance

Whatever your plans for the future of your company – an IPO, an acquisition, growing to a billion valuation and beyond – governance will be key to reaching your goal. It's much easier to get governance and good practice in place when there are just a few of you, and much harder to back-track and introduce processes when there are more of you and things are happening fast.

Say you expect to be acquired: if you have accurate records of meetings and detailed paperwork going back through all the early decisions, it will be easier for the acquirer to do their due diligence and give your books a clean bill of health. Some say you should behave like a public company from the start, and although it's time consuming and might seem like overdoing it when you're just a small start-up, deals can fall through if there are any uncertainties in your company's past.

Hence the importance of your board. They will help to ensure that the right processes are followed, and the paperwork associated with board meetings will create a record of financial reports, strategic choices, and when and how decisions were made.

There are standard processes that you must follow, but that doesn't prevent you from establishing the tone that best suits your business at board meetings. Within a few years of launching Cobra Beer, co-founders Lord Bilimoria and Arjun Reddy had built a team and established a board with non-executive directors. Their goal was to have good governance as soon as possible in order to set the standards for the company as it grew. But they also wanted their board to be part of an ecosystem supporting the company.

> Our AGMs were legendary because they were very well attended. All our shareholders would come, including our original angel investor. And we would also invite our bankers, we'd invite our advertising agency, our PR agencies – they all said, "We've never attended a client AGM before," – because we're like a family. I always believe that partnership is not just partnering with your business partner. You partner with everyone: your suppliers, your customers, your advisors, your lawyers, your accountants, your advertising agency, your PR agency. When you have that partnering approach, you get so much more out of the relationship than if it's, "You're the client, I'm the customer." It's a completely different mindset when you have a partnership mindset.
>
> Lord Bilimoria, entrepreneur

Creating the ideal board

There is no such thing as an ideal board – at least, not in the long-term. A start-up will go through many changes in the early days – it may pivot, it may need to increase the number of employees very rapidly, it may need to fire one of the co-founders – and each of these transitions might require a different mix of skills and experience on the board to help.

One way to get the mix right is to come up with your idea of a dream board for the stage you are at, and then see if your investors and others can help you bring people with the necessary attributes together. Gonçalo de Vasconcelos was able to put together the mix he needed on his board – a banker, a lawyer and an entrepreneur

– but he had to work hard and persist in order to get the people he wanted.

> We are incredibly lucky with the board of directors that we have. I wish that all companies, all start-ups, could be just as lucky.
>
> The first non-executive director to join was David Gill, who was the managing director of St John's Innovation Centre [in Cambridge]. He worked for HSBC in the past. He has been involved with venture capitalism, investment. He has been a part of St John's Innovation Centre. He kindly accepted my invitation to join as a non-executive director, and his wealth of experience and knowledge and understanding of people is crucial.
>
> The other person that joined was Tim Bellis. He's the best lecturer I had for the entire MBA course. He used to be a senior partner in Herbert Smith, the very large law firm in M&A and corporate transactions. He understands, not only the legals, but also the mentality of those deals. He has been absolutely instrumental. I asked him, actually, several times to become a non-executive director, which he passed on because he was very busy. But he retired and is now chairman at SyndicateRoom and getting more and more involved. He's very good at listening and asking all the right questions…and he challenges in a really respectful way that I absolutely love. He makes me think; that really helps.
>
> Then finally, Jonathan Milner, who invested. He didn't want to get involved because he was too busy and it's way out of his comfort zone in terms of the sectors that he invests in. Then we started delivering and he started getting more involved, or more interested. I started having coffee with him every two months, and then every month, and then every two weeks. Since then, he has become very much like Tim Bellis…a mentor of mine, and a friend of mine, as well. He brings the experience of scaling up a business. Jonathan adds value. We're able to go to him, as I just did last night with an email.

> "Look, I'm having this problem. Have you come across that before? What do you think? I'm thinking about doing this." He replied straightaway.
>
> Gonçalo de Vasconcelos, entrepreneur

Getting a stellar board is not a matter of luck. You have to make the right connections and you have to be very persuasive. The people you are targeting have to want to give up their time to help you, and you need to find a way to motivate them to do that.

> I think they enjoy doing it, because they can really see that I'm listening and I'm taking good notice of their advice. I'm following it or I'm discussing it. I'm very open about any issues we have where we might need their advice. It's a very enjoyable board because there are no egos involved. No one is there to ask questions just to show how clever they are.
>
> Gonçalo de Vasconcelos, entrepreneur

The board Chair should be chosen with care. They will play a key role in how you and the board work together as your company develops, and also in managing investors – particularly VCs. A strong Chair will know what to ask for from VCs and what to expect them to contribute, and could get more out of them than you might if you're a first-time entrepreneur.

> Having a strong Chair with prior experience of working with VCs means someone who can say, "You are going to open that door for me, and you are going to do this, and by the way, in the next funding round, this is how the allocations will look."
>
> Max Bautin, investor

A Chair or board member from one of your investors will have their eye on the bigger picture. Saul Klein of Index Ventures was AlertMe's investor director, and played an important role in spotting when the company needed to up its game to keep out the competition.

❝ There was one time when a large US company was trying to sell their energy analytics product to British Gas, and Saul said to us, "Look, they're parking their tanks on your lawn. You cannot let this stand." In a very short time, we had to set about generating our own product…and make sure we got the business, and that was very challenging. It was only thanks to Saul stiffening our spines that we did it, and I look back on that as very, very important strategic input.

Pilgrim Beart, entrepreneur

Companies like AlertMe go through various stages of growth, and the business model has to evolve as their technology and the market evolve. When this happens in your company, you will find that you may need different skills and experience on the board. What is right for a handful of employees and the early phase of intensive product development may not be right when you're looking for big customers and setting up a supply chain.

As Emily Mackay found, it can be hard to keep up when things are changing fast, and it can come as a shock when you realise how ruthless you have to be when making sure your board is fit for purpose.

❝ We changed the board completely – from the people who were in very early and supporters and mentors for me, to people who were more experienced in the industry. That was a good decision. The evolution needs to be quite fast with your advisory pool when you're growing quite fast as a company. So even 12 months in a company can change the kind of advice you need.

I don't think we evolved fast enough. I think we were not ruthless enough in what we needed to achieve and tried to take up too many contacts.

Emily Mackay, entrepreneur

Working with the board

Your board is there for three reasons: to ensure good governance, to ensure that the company operates within all the applicable standards and regulations, and to offer help and advice (whether you think you need it or not). Naturally, you will want to have a good working relationship with your board, but there could be challenges. The wrong mix of board members, failing to change the board as the company's requirements change, and ignoring advice from the board can all jeopardise your journey.

However much effort you put into recruiting the right board members – and don't forget that some board members will be selected by your investors – things may not be perfect. There could be frictions around the table, or members of the board may have different agendas they wish to pursue. If the board doesn't align on the common purpose of creating a successful company and agree on how that success will be measured, you will have to tackle the problem head on and try to make the necessary changes.

> You don't want people to be concerned with showing how clever they are. Everyone around the table is clever. We all know that. We all have to focus on building a great business.
>
> Gonçalo de Vasconcelos, entrepreneur

The relationship goes both ways. Don't be the CEO who doesn't take advice, or even acknowledge that it might be useful.

> We love to have proactive partnerships with everybody that we invest in, but you can't spend all of your time with every-one. And if there's an individual in your portfolio who isn't keen on taking advice and working with you in a proactive and co-operative way, then sometimes it's best to step back and use your energy on other companies that are.
>
> There are instances where we've had to step away from the board because, simply, you can take a horse to water but you can't make it drink. In those cases, the CEO is very unwilling to change the way they operate. That may not be around market

direction or product direction; it might be around management style or hiring. There comes a point at which, if you are not being listened to and the relationship breaks down, then sometimes it's best to step back and do what you do from the sidelines, rather than have a proactive partnership.

Luke Hakes, investor

Not all your advisors will be board members

One of the things that has been part of us making the progress we have has been the willingness to take on advice. It's always very difficult if you go ask for advice and people say, "I did such and such, and it was this and this, and I have this and this opinion," and it doesn't apply to you; then you're not learning anything. But the more you can learn from other people's experience, the more you save yourself from hurting yourself badly. It's really important to listen to advice. If you can avoid making the same mistakes as other people, then why not?

Fiona Nielsen, entrepreneur

You should be able to find plenty of people who are willing to offer advice and help if you ask for it. Getting plugged in to a network of entrepreneurs and investors is always useful, and locations that are promoted as technology or entrepreneurial clusters often have events and venues specifically designed to bring people together.

I think there is so much talent out there, so many experiences, and a sort of network of people who know people – who can find you customers, who can find you people to solve problems, who can find you great staff – and you really need to tap in to all of that.

Pilgrim Beart, entrepreneur

Another entrepreneur who has made a habit of asking for advice is Gonçalo de Vasconcelos.

> The crucial thing I've done since starting SyndicateRoom is to listen and learn. I was incredibly lucky to be surrounded by people who have been there, done that, and if they had any tips, it would be silly of me not to listen. Entrepreneurs can't act like teenagers [who think they] know everything... We have to learn as we go along. So why not listen to those people that already know?
>
> Gonçalo de Vasconcelos, entrepreneur

But when there are a lot of people willing – and trying – to help, you might find it gets too much. You need to understand what help you need, rather than accepting every offer. It's much easier for people to help you if you know what you want help with.

> I don't think entrepreneurs find it hard to ask for help; they love asking for help, and they'll take help from anyone. But they don't necessarily know what they want help with and why, and so they'll take a lot of help. They'll sometimes take up quite a lot of people's time, and then they won't be very good at deciding which help to take and what not to take. And sometimes, they can even be quite ungrateful for that help, I've found. That's not all entrepreneurs; most of them, I think, do appreciate advice that's given. But I think when you ask for help you need to be very clear on what you want help with.
>
> Jessica Dick, entrepreneur and investor

How do you know what sort of help you need? One way to gauge who to approach is to look at the stage of the business. In the very early days, you'll almost certainly need help putting together the team, and an outside observer might have a better perspective on the skills you have in place already and those you're missing.

> Very early-stage companies will typically have a set of skills or a couple of skills that are missing. The first area where they might want help is within that skillset. A good place to start is to ask what might be missing among the team that your

business needs in order to be successful, and that might be the area where you should ask for help. And then it's about asking the right person for that help.

Jessica Dick, entrepreneur and investor

But be selective. Too many offers of advice can take up too much of your time and end up not helping with your challenges.

> There was a lot of goodwill, which ended up becoming lots of meetings and coffees in my diary. Sometimes that was great, and other times it was just noise that took me away from other things. That was quite a big learning experience for me: the importance of being politely ruthless and looking after your own time.
>
> Emily Mackay, entrepreneur

The issue of time goes both ways. You, as an entrepreneur, are incredibly busy and may not have as much time as you would like to discuss your issues with your advisors, but they, too, are very busy, and you need to treat their time with as much respect as you treat your own.

> What can be difficult for investors is that, sometimes, entrepreneurs ask for a lot of help and a lot of advice, and then they don't necessarily take on that advice. Which is fine – but it can be quite disheartening for advisors, investors, mentors, anyone who's offering a lot of help, if they then see their advice disregarded. If somebody has given an entrepreneur quite a lot of time and then they've gone against the advice, the entrepreneur should at least go back to them and explain why they decided to take someone else's advice. It's a big time investment, and I've seen entrepreneurs who've done this time and time again. People give a lot of their free time and their skills and their experience, so it's good to be appreciative.
>
> Jessica Dick, entrepreneur and investor

While you will be keen to ask for help from wherever you can get it, Luke Hakes cautions that you should be wary of how you reward those that do respond to your requests.

> I often see early-stage founders collecting advisors, giving them equity because they think it's a good thing to do. Getting the best out of advisors is very challenging, and you'll soon give away quite a lot of equity if you simply offer up a piece of equity for somebody to sit on your advisory board. You'll find, in many cases, that if you do that without any strings attached, you get very little advice. So I would be frugal with the equity. I would be targeted in [selecting] any advisors, and I would be specific about my investors.
>
> Luke Hakes, investor

Mentors

The mentor relationship is slightly different to that of an advisor. You might recruit an advisor based on their specific skills and knowledge in your sector area, or to help with one aspect of your business. The mentor–entrepreneur situation is a little different: they're the person you go to with all of your problems and challenges, not just, for example, a product question.

If you're a first-time entrepreneur, a good mentor can mean the difference between success and failure. Some mentors provide their time, others provide both time and funding. Critical to the relationship is that the entrepreneur is willing to learn – as we saw in Chapter 2 – otherwise all that time and money is wasted.

Mentors do different things, too. Sometimes they are key to getting a crucial supplier relationship off the ground, or they could open doors to further funding or customers. They tend to get involved because they can see ways they can help, and because they like to see others succeed.

Business plan competitions aimed at very early-stage entrepreneurs and start-ups often progress through stages, and the later stages include mentoring in some form or other depending what is most appropriate. Some entrants will need training in giving a presentation, others might need help with their financials. Emily Mackay got mentoring support through entering a start-up competition at Anglia Ruskin University. The competition was intended to bring in external entrepreneurs to advise, and winning gave Emily not only some much-needed cash, but also some much-needed help from a mentor.

> This was the very first time I'd ever tried to do anything on my own like this, so everything was brand new. How to do the most basic things – things that I now think are laughably easy – was completely new. I didn't really understand what they meant, so I had to learn everything from scratch.
>
> Emily Mackay, entrepreneur

A mentor can make the magic happen – Lord Bilimoria's story

Lord Bilimoria's business mentor made a key introduction in the early days of Cobra Beer. The introduction, through co-founder Arjun Reddy's uncle, was a stroke of luck for the fledgling entrepreneurs.

> *We were very lucky when we were introduced to the brewery in India by our business mentor. They happened to be the biggest independent brewery in India, they happened to be really successful and, most importantly, they happened to have the best brew master in India and they didn't have a brand name... We could do it under our own brand name. The Cobra brand is our most valuable asset.*
>
> Lord Bilimoria, entrepreneur

Everything aligned. The brew master had spent six years in the Czech Republic and had obtained a PhD from Prague University, so he brought scientific rigour to developing the exact taste that Bilimoria and Reddy wanted for their new beer. Around 30 samples of bottled beer were tasted, tested and analysed in the laboratory in Bangalore. Eventually, a taste profile was established, but the recipe was very complex.

It couldn't be just a standard malted barley, yeast, water and hops. It would have to be three varieties of hops, and extra maize and rice, and eventually wheat and a double-fermented process. That's what gives Cobra its texture and its taste.

Lord Bilimoria, entrepreneur

Without the right mentor, they might not have found the right brew master with the required understanding of chemistry, and Cobra beer might have remained a dream.

The investor/mentor – David and Jonathan's story

Another mentoring relationship resulted in the creation of Abcam, a global business with a market cap of around £2.5 billion at the time of writing. Mentoring played a key role not only in getting the business off the ground, but also in helping it survive through some tough times in the early days.

David Cleevely met Jonathan Milner at a dinner party. Cleevely was a tech entrepreneur, Milner was a researcher who was fed up with his tools – and more specifically, the quality of the antibodies he needed to use for his research. Their conversation revolved around the production of antibodies, how they were distributed and what costs were involved. For Cleevely, going into the antibody business was a no-brainer, like 'a £20 note was left on the pavement', as he described it.

The combination of Cleevely's tech expertise and Milner's knowledge of the research sector was ideal on paper, but Cleevely was too busy running his own business to run another, and Milner was a scientist with no business experience whatsoever. But Milner was willing to give it a go, and mentoring was going to be crucial if he was going to switch successfully from being a researcher to being an entrepreneur.

There's a gazebo in my garden that will for ever be known as the Abcam mentoring gazebo…Every Saturday for three or four hours, I would sit there with Jonathan and talk him through how the company was going and what to do.

David Cleevely, entrepreneur and investor

David was incredibly generous with his time and mentored me through transitioning from a pure academic. I realised very early on that being an entrepreneur and trying to get a business off the ground, your mind has to flip really quickly between interviewing, doing the cashflow, trying to get customers, making sure the investors are happy...All of these things were incredibly stressful for me.

Jonathan Milner, entrepreneur and investor

The experience not only led to the stellar success of the company, but served as a model for Jonathan as he moved into investing and mentoring himself.

THREE THINGS ABOUT BOARD MEMBERS, ADVISORS AND MENTORS

- Lots of people are willing to help entrepreneurs, regardless of whether they are directly connected with the company or not.
- Try to be strategic about seeking advice: work out what you need to know and then find the right person to help. Don't simply take advice from everybody – it will waste your and their time.
- Be polite! Always thank people for their advice and suggestions, and, if you decide not to act on what they've told you, let them know why.

CHAPTER 7

Customers and product–market fit

> The number one reason why businesses don't succeed is because they fail to build a product or service that is actually solving a customer's needs.

Customers and product–market fit were one of the top three challenges for our entrepreneurs. Hardly surprising, because you're not in business if you haven't got customers, and you can't get customers if you don't have product–market fit. Among the issues our entrepreneurs mentioned were identifying and qualifying potential customers, working with customers to refine product–market fit, accessing decision-makers and the length of the sales cycle. There are plenty of things to think about as you explore how to get your product to market.

Do you know who your customers are? Sounds straightforward: they're the people who buy the product, but are they the ones that use it, or are they part of a distribution channel that you have to sell to before your product reaches the end-user? If your product has to go through one or more links to reach its point of use, your challenges will be multiplied.

Is there a market for what you plan to sell? That question should have an obvious answer, too – after all, it should be in your business plan. But all too often entrepreneurs are so taken with the brilliance of their idea that they fail to notice that nobody is interested in what they are developing. Business history is littered with ideas that never found a following.

And then, timing is everything. Sometimes the market is simply not ready for your product. Can you find a way to create a market? Can you survive until the market develops? Is your offering so good that, if you build it, they will come?

> Don't take everything on faith. Don't assume that there is a market unless you have proof there is one.
>
> Ramona Liberoff, entrepreneur and investor

Who is your customer?

You have a product. You are convinced that somewhere there is a market for it, but where? And how do you reach your customers? Finding the sweet spot of product–market fit starts with identifying your customer and the problem you will solve for them. But that is unlikely to be as straightforward as it sounds.

Who are you solving a problem for? You might think you know exactly who will buy your product, and therefore who has the problem you are solving. But do you? With consumer products, you may sell direct to the consumer via a website or bricks-and-mortar premises, but you may also sell via a channel, such as a supermarket or department store. In which case, you have to market your product both to the buyers in the channel and also to the customer – so that the buyers know there are people who want to buy your product if they stock it.

For innovative start-ups, the chances of being distracted from the problem are even greater.

> It's a challenge keeping focused on the problem in the customer/payer's mind and not becoming distracted by the coolness of the technology.
>
> Dan Cowell, entrepreneur

An associated problem is identifying who the real customers are when there's a lot of buzz about the new technology.

> You'll find a lot of interest in what you do and possibly a lot of hype about your new product or solution, especially in industries that are not used to start-ups. This will mean there will be a lot of potential customers showing interest and taking up your time. Being able to discern between the ones that are merely interested because they want to speak to the cool new start-up with the interesting technology and those that are able and willing to put their hand into their pocket to fund a purchase is a key challenge. And the earlier you can sort the wheat from the chaff, the less time you'll waste.
>
> Toby Schultz, entrepreneur

To make matters worse, your customers may change. As you develop your product, you may go from direct to channel sales, you may engage with distributors and exporters, and you may need different marketing strategies to reach different segments of the market. Changing product–market fit can be challenging if you start out fixing a problem for a small demographic and then try to move into a larger market. If you fail to adapt and grow, you won't be able to meet the needs of that larger market.

> Product–market fit is not a single point in time. As the product changes and you evolve, as you get larger, your customer base is going to change. And as your customer base changes, your product's probably going to have to change, or your services.
>
> Jon Bradford, entrepreneur and investor

Things are rarely static in the start-up world, and the sales journey is a case in point.

Identifying your customer – Toby's story

Things are complex enough if your end-user is not your customer, but the non-profit sector brings its own challenges when you're trying to create a product–market fit. As Toby Norman – co-founder of Simprints – explains, that means you need multiple feedback loops to make sure everyone involved in the multi-stage journey to end-user is kept on track.

> Something that we've seen very consistently in our work and that we find incredibly important is having really clear feedback loops for the different stakeholders in our ecosystem. You can easily imagine a normal for-profit context; essentially, your customer and your payer are the same person. If I am selling an application on the pay store that does some function, and I'm selling that directly to a consumer, if the application is good, the customer will buy it, will pay for it. That's a pretty tight feedback loop. If no one's buying my product, I know I've got to fix something.
>
> One of the challenges we have in the non-profit sector is sometimes the user and the payer aren't the same person. So, for example, our project could be funded by the Gates Foundation, but the actual implementation is being done by Mercy Corps, and it might be a manager who selects Simprints to use as their biometric frontline tool, but it will be a health worker – potentially in a village thousands of miles from there – who's actually the one using Simprints at the end of the day. And the beneficiary, who is actually receiving the service, has nothing to do with any of that, except their interaction with the health worker.
>
> So in order for us to stay effective, we've really got to think: what are our feedback loops with every single one of those stakeholders? Obviously, with the payer, it's a financial feedback loop, and that's often the strong one that a lot of people in this space focus on. But I think there's a real risk that if you just focus on that financial feedback loop, you are actually going to miss the hugely important user feedback loop to the health worker and the impact feedback loop to the beneficiary. If you don't have those things, you are not going to be learning and you're

not going to be continuously improving the work you do. I think that's fundamental, because this area is too complicated for anyone to be able to predict how everything's going to go first time round. You have to have those feedback loops, so you can learn, so you can improve. That's what it takes to create impact at scale.

Toby Norman, entrepreneur

Defining the core customer – Emily's story

In the early days, having more than one type of customer may simply be the result of getting sales where you can. That's a natural response to the need to generate income, but it can have disadvantages. With her first company, Emily Mackay found that problems defining and focusing on her core customers impacted on her efforts to raise Series A funding.

We had experimented with product–market fits, but in the eyes of investors we hadn't quite got it. At the time, appetite was for Series A companies to have a very clear product–market fit, and where we were selling, there wasn't sufficient replicability.

We had quite a range of customers. We had consumer-level relationships with relatively small but recurring amounts of money – so monthly subscriptions. And then we'd also done bigger deals – more like consultancy, one-off chunks of cash. The challenge was that it wasn't clear which we were and which was actually going to be replicable.

I think, in hindsight, if I was to be in that position again, I would treat product–market fit as a hypothesis to be tested very rapidly. And you have to keep changing the hypothesis as you learn more. I think we were too slow to take that testing approach.

Towards the end of the company, we had a completely different idea of how we could commercialise the information and we started testing that out. But we'd run out of runway before we really completed the tests thoroughly.

Emily Mackay, entrepreneur

The takeaway for Emily was the need to be ruthless about testing product–market fit, and to fix a strict time limit during which the fit would be proved or disproved.

For instance, "I hypothesise that this market requires this value at this price, and the way of delivering it will be this." And, of course, you have to do that on a really lean basis because you don't have money to burn if it doesn't work.

Emily also understood that the results should not be viewed through rose-tinted spectacles. It's all too easy to be so passionate about your idea that you ignore any negative feedback, but it is often the negative feedback that teaches you the most.

Don't be optimistic in the way you view the results. Be very pessimistic, because then you can iterate quite quickly and work out whether there is value in the thing you've created. Better yet, if you already have pull from the market, you're trying to find a solution to a problem. That's the ideal.

Emily Mackay, entrepreneur

The importance of listening to customers

❝ Speak to five potential customers every week.

Jon Bradford, entrepreneur and investor

How do you establish product–market fit? By listening to your customers. If you don't, you risk developing a product that you like but nobody will buy – we can't say this often enough.

❝ The thing that good start-ups could and should be doing all the time is being incredibly customer-focused and thinking about what the problem is you're trying to solve. And that's not what's happening between your ears and what you think is happening. It's what you learn when you're listening to potential customers. I'm a great believer that people should speak to potential customers, one a day, every day. So in any given week, you speak to five potential customers.

Jon Bradford, entrepreneur and investor

Everybody in the team should be speaking to customers, including the CEO. If you do this, you greatly reduce the risk of failing to find a product–market fit. And, as Jon Bradford points out, listening to customers is the only way to steer your start-up in the right direction, since your original ideas will inevitably change and evolve.

> The more customer-centric you become, the more conversations you can have and the greater the likelihood you will find a way through – because the thing you think you're going to do and the thing that you will do are two different things.
>
> Jon Bradford, entrepreneur and investor

The listening brand – Lord Bilimoria's story

Getting your product off the ground is a very difficult stage. You have zero credibility, nobody knows you, nobody knows your product, nobody knows your brand. Why should they buy from you? Why should they supply you? Why should they finance you when you have zero credibility? I believe they do those things if you have passion and faith and confidence and believe in yourself, in your brand, in your product. That gives them the faith to trust you, to give you a chance.

Lord Bilimoria, entrepreneur

Cobra Beer relied on feedback from customers in the early days in order to get that crucial product–market fit and build the brand.

I first contacted the brewery in September and the product was available in June...and from June to December, we had six months of getting feedback from the marketplace and tweaking the product to get it right based on feedback.

Lord Bilimoria and his co-founder Arjun Reddy went around in a battered old car, which needed push-starting every day, carrying 15 cases of beer at a time. They would go into restaurants and ask the managers to buy their unknown beer. But the restaurants weren't keen. There was competition from the already well-established Kingfisher beer and Carlsberg – far more familiar to the clientele of Indian restaurants in the UK at the time.

One thing that Lord Bilimoria discovered about selling Cobra in the early days was that he wasn't selling to the restaurateurs, he was selling to their customers. There was a difference between direct and end customers, and he had to persuade the people in the middle – the restaurateurs – that he cared about their customers as much as they did.

I learned very early from the restaurateurs that they put their customers first. They said, "It doesn't matter about us. If you say your beer is so good, leave a couple of bottles, we'll try it with our regulars. If our regulars like it, we'll put in our first order. If our wider customers like it, we'll reorder."

The chance was all they needed. It wasn't long before Cobra was proving popular with the restaurant clientele. But Bilimoria and Reddy couldn't continue to grow their sales in the way they'd got started: one old car that could carry 15 cases could not keep pace with the growth they were after.

From day one, we got 99% re-ordering. It was phenomenal. That gives you the confidence to extrapolate into a global brand, but then you've got to get distributors to stock it. Once we got the top 100 restaurants in London selling our beer, the distributors noticed. They show interest, then you get the big distributors and you grow your distribution.

But Bilimoria's strategy was bigger even than that. He wanted Cobra beer available wherever consumers wanted to buy it – and that meant getting supermarkets on board as well – and then to start exporting.

My strategy was always that consumers would discover Cobra in the restaurants. Today, Cobra is available in over 98% of all licensed Indian restaurants in the UK. It's also available in just about all the supermarkets, and off licences and cash-and-carry stores. And now, increasingly, in hundreds of Turkish, Lebanese, Thai and Chinese restaurants, and in gastro pubs, restaurants and hotels. And we export to 40 countries around the world.

And all this was achieved with no money for marketing in the early days. They didn't have money for branded beer glasses or any point-of-sale items, apart from a table tent card in the Cobra colours

– green and black – telling the story of the brand. Bilimoria calls it a 'breakthrough' strategy.

> *How would I, even if I'm a great salesman, get my product on the shelves of a top supermarket chain? The bottles would have gathered dust because no-one would have known my product. First, I had to get people to know and like my product. And the foundation we built through word of mouth, through the restaurants where people discovered our product, gave us a very loyal following. And then we got into supermarkets, and then eventually we were able to do mainstream advertising, then eventually we were able to do things like cinema and television.*

Bilimoria recognises that, had there been the money in the company for 'shortcuts' to jump over the normal growth stages of a B2C company, they might not have worked. The value for them was the story of the brand and how it grew organically, and that remains at the core of Cobra marketing.

> *Even now when we advertise, we're very careful never to commercialise the brand, to always make sure it's the voice of Cobra from those early days when people discovered it at the grassroots.*

> Lord Bilimoria, entrepreneur

Working with large organisations

Securing a lead customer is a key factor in the success of many start-ups. Working with a major organisation to develop and refine your product helps to ensure that you focus on the all-important customer problem and gives you credibility in the sector. The collaboration serves as an endorsement – a seal of approval for your company. It also helps you on the rocky road to profitability.

Many entrepreneurs want the kind of sales they can get through large organisations, like supermarkets if they're in the food sector, for example, or utilities if they're in the smart meter space. But there are various hurdles to overcome.

6 When I bring together the leaders of large businesses and the leaders of start-ups, I find that there needs to be some common

understanding of language and how to work really closely together. Start-ups I work with are often trying to get into a large organisation to partner with them or to get them as a customer. What they struggle with is how to navigate their way around a large organisation, how to communicate effectively, and to understand what large organisations are looking for from them in terms of success criteria and what measures they might use.

Bridget Connell, investor

Large organisations have processes and structures that sometimes make it hard for their employees to work with start-ups. They may have to ring-fence a team of people to collaborate with you from a distance, or find a way for you to go in and work with them on site, and managers might have to give staff time to work with you along-side their other tasks. Even if solutions can be found, there may be financing issues that make it difficult to bill the work internally.

Sometimes, I mentor entrepreneurs who are running a pilot or trial working alongside a large organisation. It can fail or stall because full-time employees in the large organisation have not got the right project code or the right billable hours to allow them to work with the entrepreneurs. There needs to be slightly more relaxed ways of working to allow those two things to work more effectively.

Bridget Connell, investor

There are also practical issues around size and sustainability. Large organisations may not want to risk working with a start-up that doesn't have a track record because they fear it won't survive. Provisions such as the Small Business Research Initiative in the UK – designed to promote interactions between the public sector and innovative companies – go some way to ameliorating this problem, but the issue remains a challenge for many start-ups.

We've had problems in terms of getting contracts, being a new start-up and persuading big companies to trust us. You need to go through procurement, RFPs, and due diligence. Then they go, "You're only two years old. We don't work with start-ups that size."

Elin Haf Davies, entrepreneur

Sometimes you shouldn't take 'no' for an answer – Priya's story

Priya Lakhani launched fresh ethnic sauce brand Masala Masala as a first-time entrepreneur with no experience of the food sector or manufacturing, and no experience of sales. But what she had was the tenacity to pursue her vision. It would have been all too easy to give up after the first few knock-backs, but she kept going and secured two very important lead customers.

I drove to Waitrose. I drove to the head office, went into reception. "I've got this for the buyer." I knew the buyer's name, and they said, "You can leave it in reception." I said, "No, these are fresh. If I leave them with you, they'll go off. I've sent these over about five times. Each time I send them to Waitrose, I have to send them in a chilled vehicle, every time I send a chilled vehicle, it costs me 60 pounds. It's not like sending something in the post. So, I need her to take these. I will only leave if she takes them face to face."

Priya Lakhani, entrepreneur

Priya was true to her word and sat outside the buyer's office until she had seen her and handed over the samples. Her instinct was right; a few days later, Waitrose confirmed they wanted to launch Priya's sauces. But even if the buyer had said no, at least Priya would have got some feedback and been able to modify her sauces to suit the buyer's – and, ultimately, their customers' – preferences.

It's very, very difficult to say no to a human being, but it's very easy to say no to an email. At least if they want to say no, they'll hear you out. Then they'll justify their "no" with a "because", because only the most assertive people just say no.

Priya Lakhani, entrepreneur

Timing

> ❛ Come hell or high water, you have to exist until the market is
> ready.
>
> Ronjon Nag, entrepreneur and investor

Timing is more important for some sectors than for others,
although it can play a role in break-out successes that happen to
coincide with external drivers. For instance, Priya Lakhani and her
ethnic sauces may have benefited from a wave of interest in Indian
cooking or a TV series set in one of the countries her sauces rep-
resented, but essentially it was about producing good sauces that
people liked and wanted to buy, and the timing wasn't so crucial.

Technology innovators, on the other hand, are much more
impacted by timing. Their technology might rely on other innova-
tions that haven't quite caught up yet, or might be so different from
what customers are used to that they resist the change. You've probably heard about products that were too far ahead of their time,
such as: the Apple Newton and Palm Pilot, which were precursors
to tablet computers; the Palm Treo, which pre-dated the iPhone;
and any number of social media sites that couldn't get the kind of
traction that Facebook later achieved.

For some innovators, it can be a matter of hanging in there until
the market comes around, but that is very difficult to do when
you're short of cash and bills have to be paid.

> ❛ If you're an innovator, you're delivering a new product to a
> new market, you're probably going to be a bit early for the
> market. So the question is: how do you survive?
>
> Pilgrim Beart, entrepreneur

Ronjon Nag learnt how difficult it was when he was struggling to
keep his company going after a major down round, and in a market
that was growing very slowly but showed every sign of developing
significantly if only they could survive. Finally, they secured a key
contract with Sprint, which was the breakthrough they needed, and

ultimately went on to be acquired by Research in Motion (RIM) – developers of the Blackberry.

> A lesson I give companies is, "You have to exist. If you believe your concept is there, but there's a market timing risk – and often there is because, by definition, you're innovating and the market may not realise they want your product or your company – you have to pace yourself and exist. Come hell or high water, you have to exist until the market wants you and is ready."
>
> Ronjon Nag, entrepreneur and investor

How do you continue to exist if the market isn't ready for you? By being very careful with your cash. Ronjon Nag's company went from 70 to 7 employees when costs had to be slashed in order to break even. When things started to improve and the big contracts came in, for a while he says they were 'so traumatised from having no money we didn't spend it'.

> It's not impossible to chart a path...[but]...you'll have to remain extremely thrifty until the market emerges. There's nothing wrong with being early as long as you haven't spent every penny in the bank before the market is there.
>
> Ramona Liberoff, entrepreneur and investor

How to succeed when you're early to market – Pilgrim's story

Pilgrim Beart has form when it comes to being early to market. At least three of the companies that he has been involved with have launched innovative technology that required a highly strategic approach in order to define and develop a market. The first two – ActiveRF and Splash Power – eventually failed, but all the lessons Pilgrim took on board from those two experiences helped to inform his eventual success with AlertMe.

ActiveRF went through various applications of their radio-frequency identification (RFID) product until they focused efforts on commercial anti-theft systems. Pilgrim and his team thought they were doing well when they were granted a trial with a large supermarket – and today, RFID is found on thousands of items, including things that are popular targets for shop-lifters such as razor blades – but at the time, the supermarket trial proved a poisoned chalice.

> I think we never really managed to get that product–market fit. And what became our main customers, which were large supermarkets, are very tough customers. It's very easy to get stuck in trials with them, and never actually close the big deal. And meanwhile, you're running out of cash. So we just never really hit our stride.
>
> Pilgrim Beart, entrepreneur

Splash Power was also too early to market and struggled to find the right application for their product. The idea was ahead of its time, as Pilgrim points out.

> Splash Power was a wireless power start-up, started by a couple of people who were fresh graduates out of Cambridge. Fantastic individuals. And their vision was that we could charge all of the gadgets in our life by just throwing them onto something that looked a bit like a mouse mat. And as if by magic, they would charge up.
>
> It was a fantastic vision, and obviously it is now coming true. But now is 2018, not 2002 when they started. We were very early to market – we were probably ten years before the market really emerged – and we kept trying to deliver the end game, which was the mass market consumer product.
>
> It's very hard to put technology into mass market products like smartphones. There's no space, there's no formal budget. So that was a challenging thing to do. And ultimately Splash Power was fire sold in 2008.

As always, there were lessons to be learned.

> I think, in retrospect, what we could have done was to aim at a slightly less ambitious target and focus on niche markets which really needed

wireless charging, like military or sports. The company could easily have survived within those niches and continued to develop.

Among the challenges Pilgrim faced with early smart meter innovator AlertMe was that of building the product before a supply chain had evolved to serve the sector, and then later how to outsource non-core activities and focus on what made the company valuable to their customers.

There's a massive opportunity for you to grow as the market grows, but what are the dynamics of that? For me, a key thing is that, in the early days, you will have to do all sorts of things that you don't really want to do and that perhaps you're not very good at.

AlertMe is a classic example. We had to design and build hardware at scale in order to deliver a complete solution to our customers.

By delivering a complete solution to their customers, AlertMe had the opportunity to work with those customers to understand their needs and refine the product they were offering.

We got that product in the hands of B2C customers in the UK initially, which was fantastic for co-creation: we could learn from them, understand what was needed to fix the technology and to fix the proposition and iterate.

Refining the product led to more interest, and the market started to develop, meaning that AlertMe could outsource the parts of their solution that were not their differentiators.

We didn't want to be a hardware vendor, but in the early days, there's no one else to work with. As a market takes off, there are other people to work with, and it's really important that you start to work with them and that you partner with people. You can offload parts of your solution to them, bits that you didn't really want to do anyway – like hardware, in the case of AlertMe.

But also, you'll find increasingly that you can buy a piece of your solution from other vendors. It's really important that you re-engineer to ensure that you can ride on those scaling curves as well, because if you don't, you'll end up trying to be good at everything, and nobody can be good at everything – not even Amazon or Apple. And it's important that you focus on the piece you're going to be good at; make sure you are world class at it, and that you are very good at working with others.

That kind of dynamic is what makes ecosystems happen. But it's very important to understand when that's happening in your market, and to proactively divest yourself of all the bits that you had to do in the beginning for practical reasons but which are not really core to your excellence.

Eventually, British Gas came on board as a customer, but that took tenacity.

I spent nearly two years driving 150 miles on an almost weekly basis down to Staines to try and win British Gas as a customer.

Pilgrim's hard work paid off, and the process highlighted some of the issues that small start-ups face.

It's very challenging to win a very large customer like that. It's very hard to work with very large companies if you're a small start-up. But I think what we ended up doing – which was perhaps luck more than strategy – was that we were able to use the engagement we had got from our direct B2C customers to prove to these large channel partners – like British Gas, and Lowe's in the US – that the technology did work, the proposition did work. People would pay us money, even if was only on a small scale, in the hundreds and thousands of customers. That was the kind of evidence that gave them faith to commit to it, and British Gas really did commit.

Pilgrim Beart, entrepreneur

Subsequently British Gas became an investor, and eventually acquired AlertMe outright. The AlertMe technology now forms part of its Hive smart home solution.

Creating a market by creating a platform – Dominic's story

Dominic's company, Atelier Technology, is the world's first software-as-a-service (SaaS) play in jewellery. His original idea was around product development and sourcing in order to attract buyers and designers in jewellery companies, but what gradually emerged was the opportunity for a platform that brought all the players in the sector together. However, this is what Dominic describes as a chicken-and-egg-problem. If your platform is for both sides to interact and work together, how do you get them all there in the first place?

> We are a B2B service that is aimed at SME and above, so we're not really aimed at small independent stores or sole traders. We're into large retailers, brands, wholesalers and export-grade manufacturers. The SaaS play is really a solution to a chicken-and-egg problem, which is that we want to be the enterprise network in jewellery. But how do you build a network? The inherent problem in a network is how do you get two sides to come at the same time to something that they have no reason to come to until the other side is there? So that's the chicken-and-egg problem.
>
> Dominic Hill, entrepreneur

For Dominic, the key was finding ways to solve problems that his customers on all sides of the sector perhaps didn't know they had. The industry acknowledged that it typically took around 200 days for a new jewellery product to go from design to distribution, but Dominic knew that could be shortened dramatically. He felt strongly that, once all sides of the sector saw the benefits of faster, more efficient working, that would bring them to his platform.

> By providing people with a compelling reason to use your software every day – because it saves them having to put pictures in spreadsheets, or it saves them having to migrate data from PDF quotes into their internal system, or it enables them to compare two vendors' quotes instantly without having to do any work – then you're giving them a reason to log in to your website. And if you can do that on both sides of the fence simultaneously, then you've got the beginnings of a network, which is what we see with Atelier today.

Dominic not only faced the issue of creating a platform and network where none existed before, but he also had to rely on a radical change to the way in which companies bought and used software.

> Traditional enterprise software was sold via an IT guy, and then the IT guy told the people in the company that they had to use it. If you look

at HubSpot or Box or any of the great software plays – SaaS plays that have mostly come out of California – they flip the model. So now you get the users to want your product, and then they basically tell the IT guy that they want this. And the IT guy is just now doing a due diligence exercise and he's no longer the gatekeeper that he was before. It's users driving adoption.

Dominic Hill, entrepreneur

Retailers, brands, manufacturers and wholesalers in the jewellery sector have bought in to Dominic's vision, with over 500 international clients signing up in the first year since launch, including more than 75% of Mumbai's diamond exporters. A funding round in 2018 resulted in investment from a consortium led by Swarovski, and in 2019 the company planned to open an office in China and release a Chinese version of its software.

THREE THINGS ABOUT CUSTOMERS AND PRODUCT–MARKET FIT

- Talking to your customers and finding out what problems they have that you can solve is key.
- Understand the shape and stage of the market you are targeting. If you're early, then your strategy must reflect this, and talking to customers will be even more important.
- Understand who your end customer is and how you can reach them.

CHAPTER 8

Intellectual Property

> The value creation part of the business was the intellectual property.

What is intellectual property – better known as IP? The World Intellectual Property Organisation (WIPO) defines intellectual property as 'creations of the mind, such as inventions; literary and artistic works; designs; and symbols, names and images used in commerce'.

The most recognised ways to protect IP are patents and trademarks, along with copyright, industrial designs and – in some jurisdictions – utility models. All of these require registration, a fee, and certification of some kind from a recognised body to confirm that they are unique and originated with you and/or your business. According to WIPO, 3.17 million patents were filed in 2017, 12.39 million classes of trademarks were covered in 9.11 million applications, and 1.24 million designs were filed. Utility models are similar to patents but have less stringent requirements and cover a shorter time period, and 1.76 million were filed in 2017.

However, for the entrepreneur, IP actually encompasses more than this because it is what drives value in the business, and value drivers can be many things. IP is what gives a business a competitive advantage, because it is what makes the business different. For your business, this might include IP that comes under the WIPO definition, such as your product or your brand; but it might also include less tangible aspects of the business, such as the way you do things or the skills of your employees.

For instance, if you are establishing a software business, then the value drivers will include not only the code itself, but also the know-how of the people building the code. If you open a shop or restaurant, your value drivers will include your brand, and also what you do to gain an edge over your competitors – the service and ambience of the premises, for example, or the skills of your buyers in selecting the right goods for your clientele, or the recipes and expertise of your kitchen staff.

You need to identify the value drivers for your business because these are the things that you need to protect in whatever way is most appropriate. You may well have value drivers that need patent or other certified protection, but you may also find that part of protecting your IP might be preserving the goodwill associated with your brand or maintaining a company culture that helps you attract and retain the best talent.

Once you have identified the value drivers for your business, you'll be in a position to develop an IP strategy to protect them. In this chapter, we'll look at the issues surrounding patents and other ways of certifying IP. But always keep in mind that your business will have other value drivers that should be taken into account in your overall IP strategy.

Trade secrets

Some companies have built their success on creating something intangible which, although it cannot be quantified or otherwise certified, distinguishes their product and separates it from competitors. The Coca-Cola brand is a classic example of building a highly valuable brand on a trade secret.

The recipe for Coca-Cola syrup – which bottlers then mix with carbonated water to produce the drinks – is not protected by any patents. But there is apparently only one paper copy of the recipe in existence, and it is so important to the company that it is kept in a bank vault. Legend also has it that only two Coca-Cola employees know the recipe at any one time. Apparently, when one dies, the other recruits a successor and passes the recipe on.

This is, of course, somewhat preposterous. However, Coca-Cola's secret recipe is not only protected physically, but also by over a century of brand-building that has brought it to mythical status, something impossible for a new competitor entering the market to match. Coca-Cola has captured the 'secret recipe' space and competitors have to come up with some other way of differentiating their products. The contribution of the recipe to Coca-Cola's brand value is hard to quantify but most, if not all, analysts regard it as significant. The 2018 global brand rankings from Interbrand placed Coca-Cola at fifth, with a brand value of over $66 billion, and one of only two non-tech brands in the top ten, the other being McDonalds at number ten. Pepsi, a cola brand without a secret recipe, was ranked 22, with a value of around $20 billion. Coca-Cola, McDonalds and Pepsi are the only three food and beverage brands in the top 30, all the rest are familiar tech and automotive names such as Apple, Amazon, Mercedes and Toyota.

You may not be keen to go to the same extremes as Coca-Cola to keep your product's secrets safe, but you will need to think carefully about whether and what level of protection you need. The value of trade secrets relies on a number of things, the most obvious being, of course, that they are kept secret and not revealed to your competitors. This in turn relies on things like the integrity of your employees, your ability to retain them and company culture. So, protecting a trade secret is not really as simple as locking it away in a bank vault.

Trademarks

Trademarks are inexpensive and relatively easy to obtain. They are particularly important in protecting intangible assets such as a brand and, apart from the name of the brand, can also cover images associated with the name and the colour(s) used for logos – the Starbucks mermaid and the particular shade of green the company uses, for example. Other assets that can be trademarked include designs (such as the Burberry check) and characters (such as Mickey Mouse or Luke Skywalker). Services may be protected with an equivalent known as a service mark. In total, there are 45 different classes of trademark recognised internationally – with ten of those relating to services – and trademarks may have to be taken out in each country or economic zone where you plan to trade.

With a trademark, you have a means of enforcement should another company or person use a name, logo, colour or other identifier that could confuse consumers and create the impression that they were buying something from your company when that isn't the case. Similarly, websites with domain names very close to recognised brands could be mistaken for the 'real' thing. Thus, there are commercial and reputational risks when a brand is mistakenly or maliciously copied, and where most or all of the value of the business is in the brand, you will need to defend it.

Some companies are well-known for the rigour with which they protect their brand – for instance, the UK's easyGroup, which began with low-cost airline EasyJet in 1995. Since then, the Group has grown the 'easy' brand, and in 2018 was estimated to hold over 1,000 registered trademarks globally using the 'easy' name. The value for the easyGroup is its brands, which it licenses to partners to commercialise, and so the Group protects its brand fiercely and fights any trademark infringements wherever it finds them.

As the easyGroup states on their website, 'Some people think they can make a fast buck by stealing our name and our reputation.' The company claims that there are two reasons why people use the 'easy' name: to gain customers by creating the impression that they are part of the Group, or to be paid to stop using the name. As a means of deterring others, the Group's website describes recent cases where they have defended the brand and won. These include a small air cargo operation in Bangladesh that called itself 'easyFly' and French supermarket giant Carrefour, which branded some of its smaller stores with the same orange colour and font used by the easyGroup. Adopting the name 'easyoffices' cost the owners of serviced office company Regus £65,000 when it had to cover the easyGroup's legal costs, while other instances never get to court because the easyGroup keeps a close eye on trademark applications and objects to any filings that they believe infringe on their brand before the application can be approved.

Do I need a patent?

There are different opinions on the necessity and benefits of patents. Certainly, if you're in tech, you will need to think about filing patents, but there are plenty of things to consider before you do so.

Will filing patents improve your chances of securing funding, or are they too expensive? Do you risk making your technology public when you should be keeping it secret while you develop and refine it? Can you afford to file patents in one or more jurisdictions, and can you afford to maintain them? How might you cope if another company infringes your patents? Can you afford litigation?

Patents are about defending your IP and possibly putting you in a better position for an exit, but they incur both known and unknown costs. Not every start-up needs to protect its IP, and the level of protection needed also varies.

> There is no clear and definitive answer; it always depends on the circumstances. But there are a few general truths. It's rarely bad to have more IP protection, as opposed to less IP protection. More IP tends to raise the value of companies, even if it's low quality IP.
>
> Zeev Fisher, entrepreneur

Some sectors – such as medical devices, drug discovery and biotech – need rigorous IP protection. Most of the value of the company can lie in its IP, and the better the patents, the higher the valuation will likely be.

Software is a little different, and there is a wide variation in how software can be protected across jurisdictions. In the UK, for example, code can be copyrighted, whereas in the US, it can sometimes – but not always – be patented. Even when software can be patented, its very nature means the filing may well be a borderline case. If this is so, you need to ask yourself whether the value of any possible protection is worth it.

> To answer this question, you have to think about what exactly you are trying to achieve. Are you going to draft and file a patent now so you can stop other companies from creating the same technology? If that's what you're thinking, then you'll probably be disappointed, because no software patent in a borderline field would ever stop anyone from doing anything.
>
> Zeev Fisher, entrepreneur

Part of the issue is that, since there are so many patents in this grey area, innovators are highly unlikely to trawl through them all to see if what they are doing has been done before – not least because such patents are very hard to read and understand.

The situation can change. In the early days of a start-up, keeping things secret might be the cheapest and most sensible way to go. But as the product develops and you start to engage with customers, you might need more protection.

> If you've got a patentable technology, you might just keep it to yourself. We've certainly had that conversation. One of our investments has some incredible technology to improve patient engagement and speed up the time it takes to assemble cohorts of patients for clinical trials. The founder wanted to patent the technology, but I said, "No, just don't tell anyone," and that's the decision we've taken – for now.
>
> Chris Smith, investor

Alex Schey cautions against patenting too early. As you grow and your technology matures, your strategy becomes clearer and you have a better chance of making the right decisions over whether and what to patent because you understand its value to the company better.

> We filed two patents at the end of 2013, and within about a year or two, our technology had superseded what was in those patents and they were worthless to us. If you can stay in tech stealth mode for a while – and there are risks associated with that, of course – and patent when your strategy is clearer and your technology more mature, I think there's a lot more value in doing it then.
>
> Alex Schey, entrepreneur

However, Victor Christou and his co-founders at Opsys took a different view. Their IP strategy was to build a portfolio of patents around the initial technology as quickly as they could. Coupled with additional IP, such as process know-how, this created a robust position. Victor likens it to playing Go, with the objective of capturing as much territory in the space as cheaply as possible, and then working out what is most valuable to the business.

> Patents won't stop competitors, but they slow them down by acting as speed bumps on the road to commercialisation.
>
> Victor Christou, entrepreneur and investor

For fire life protection company Plumis, filing the first patent was almost simultaneous with forming the company and going into a business incubator. But as the technology developed, it wasn't always essential – or possible – to file patents each time the product iterated into something slightly different.

> We initially started with our tap-mounted sprinkler, and very quickly moved on to thinking about a wall-mounted version. Our latest product is the SmartScan system. So we've tried a

number of things and sometimes it wasn't protectable, and in other cases we've let it slip because it's just been unnecessary since we've ended up with something else.

Yusuf Muhammad, entrepreneur

As with everything else, it's a judgement call. As Chris Smith indicates, he is not entirely opposed to patents. He just believes that the decision to patent something is important and should not be taken lightly.

> There's nothing wrong with patents per se, but it's not something you have to do.

Chris Smith, investor

Intellectual property and investors

Zeev Fisher feels that neither entrepreneurs nor investors pay enough attention to IP. Investors are far more interested in sales and marketing strategies, so the entrepreneurs focus on getting these right in their business plan. Whether or not the product is protected often receives much less attention.

> In my opinion, patents are not subject to proper due diligence in most angel rounds in the UK. Most angels don't treat them properly, don't get opinions on them – they look at other things.
>
> Everyone recognises IP is important, but it lives on the sidelines…"Do you have patents? Yes. Carry on." That's as much attention as IP usually gets. It's a box that needs to be ticked, which is the source of many problems.

Zeev Fisher, entrepreneur

But patents – or some form of IP protection – are particularly important in some sectors, and so founders need to think hard about how it fits into their funding strategy.

> I think that the first question a start-up CEO needs to ask themselves is: "Would drafting more patents help me to

> achieve short-term goals such as getting funding?" And that
> depends, for example, on the type of investor that you're look-
> ing to recruit.
>
> Zeev Fisher, entrepreneur

You need to know what sort of investor you are targeting because
patents cost money. While some investors might not look at you
until you have a solid set of patents in place, others may not care.
If you think your most likely investors will be the latter, then your
money could perhaps be spent on better things.

However, if patents are a key part of your value creation, then
you need to have solid defensibility. Investor Nathan Hill includes
IP as one of his top five things to look at when considering an
investment.

> What's the thing that's going to stop everybody else doing the
> same thing? Is there something in their technology? Is there
> something in their business model that stops people just cop-
> ying them and beating them to it?
>
> Nathan Hill, entrepreneur and investor

For some entrepreneurs, the thought of describing their technology in detail to investors who may never put any money into the
company is worrying. But investors can't make a sensible decision
about funding you if they don't have enough information.

> The thing I find most difficult with entrepreneurs is secrecy.
> There's no point in having a business plan and trying to
> raise money if you decide you can't reveal how the technol-
> ogy works, for example. You can't persuade me to write out a
> cheque for any amount without being able to answer, "How
> is this going to work, what is it going to do, and who or what
> problem are you trying to address?"
>
> David Gammon, investor

You might think that the only option is to ask potential investors to sign a non-disclosure agreement – an NDA – but you need to understand the investors' position on this.

> If I hear the word "NDA", I know I'm not going to make an investment – because I couldn't sign hundreds of NDAs every year and then police them. I can't remember what I had for lunch yesterday, let alone what someone told me a year ago, two years ago, five years ago.
>
> David Gammon, investor

One exception might be if there is IP that needs patent protection but it hasn't yet been filed. If you intend to file a patent in the near future, you might consider a short-term NDA until the filing is made. That way, you deal with any investor concerns about defensibility going forward. However, again looking at David's point above, investors are unlikely to want to sign such short-term NDAs any more often than they absolutely have to, so be prepared to argue your case if that is the way you want to go.

If you're looking for investment in a software product, things may be different. Here, there is an issue of whether the software is patentable at all and in which jurisdiction. It is imperative to explore your options in this case – as mentioned before, the patenting regime for software is different in the US to many other countries. However, if you are not planning to – or are unable to – patent your software, then you have to be able to make a clear case as to why investors should be interested.

> You've got to be able to explain what your software does, how it works, what it's going to address and what's unique about it. If you can't do that, it's not going to work.
>
> David Gammon, investor

Defending your registered intellectual property

Defending IP that has been registered in the form of patents or another type of recognised certification can get very expensive.

Technology companies are particularly concerned with patents and the challenges of defending them.

> I'm very conflicted because, if you are a small business and you do have a patent, the only way that patent is of value is if you sue somebody who has infringed it and win. If, say, Mercedes decided to copy us and we felt they'd infringed on our intellectual property, there's very little that we can do.
>
> Alex Schey, entrepreneur

Even when there's a clear infringement, enforcing the patent and the subsequent litigation could cost hundreds of thousands of dollars, if not millions. In the US, there are companies that will take on patent litigation for a percentage of the proceeds, but this brings its own set of problems and burdens for the business, not least in terms of the time taken up.

The issue is that patents are published, so any of your competitors can get a good look at what you're doing, and see if you've come up with ideas that they might not have thought about.

> If you register a patent, anyone in the world can go to the patent registry; they can see what you've registered and see your methodology, so you have exposed a lot of your thinking. And that means two things can happen. One is that other companies can think their way round the patent, which, if they've got enough smart people, they generally can. The other is people may litigate. If you're taking on the big tech companies, you've got an amazing new method of doing something that they do, they'll see it and you have no cash, you can't fight.
>
> Chris Smith, investor

One way to mitigate this problem is to make sure that you patent wisely in the first place.

> A patent puts your technology in the public domain, so you need to be sure that infringements can be identified very

easily. Clear infringements are much easier to defend than more ambiguous situations where the infringement is not so obvious. At Opsys, we patented a molecular structure that was very easy to identify and therefore very easy to defend.

Victor Christou, entrepreneur and investor

What if I want to sell in overseas markets?

Protecting IP overseas is an important part of any international marketing strategy, and adds several layers of complexity because, not surprisingly, regulations and standards vary widely.

In the US, the conditions for patenting software have tightened, but it may still be easier to patent software in the US than in Europe or the UK. Indeed, some things that are not patentable in the UK can still be patented in the US, and since companies that build software products are very likely to go to the US as their main market, getting the right advice is critical.

Some countries, including Brazil, China, Germany and Japan, now award an IP right called a utility model. It sits somewhere between a patent and a design, and relates to function. It also tends to be granted more quickly. Sometimes it's the best protection for products with a shape and form, such as a medical device, and companies intending to go into the Chinese market should file utility models if appropriate, rather than rely on patents. Zeev Fisher believes this is an issue companies need to focus on more closely.

UK applicants don't file utility models even when they go to China. That's a mistake. Why don't they file utility models? Because a similar right does not exist in the UK. It's just not something that the local patent profession is used to advising on. If I don't know about it and I don't do it domestically, I don't think about it when it comes to overseas protection.

Zeev Fisher, entrepreneur

How do you address this issue? By choosing a firm of patent lawyers that has an in-house international department (and so are aware of, and tuned in to, international variations) or by going to a local firm in the market you're hoping to enter.

How much should I pay for my patents?

> I've yet to see a single funding round fail because the investors have thought that the patent firm which drafted the patent applications was not reputable enough.
>
> Zeev Fisher, entrepreneur

According to IP attorney Zeev Fisher, most entrepreneurs tend to overpay for their IP protection. They believe that having the 'right' firm draft their patents will sway investors in their favour. But as we've mentioned, some investors aren't even interested in your patents, so going for the most expensive firm of patent attorneys is not necessarily money well spent. The bigger firms may have all the right mechanisms in place to process your applications correctly and on time, but many smaller sized firms employ equally good attorneys – some of whom may have experience in the larger firms – and provide better value for money since there are big disparities in costs between firms.

> If you work with someone who used to be a partner in a big firm and now works for a smaller firm, they don't stop being good just because they moved to work for a different firm.
>
> Zeev Fisher, entrepreneur

Costs can mount up, too. What starts out as a few thousand pounds for the initial patent can go up to tens of thousands over the long term due to maintenance and/or renewal fees.

Once you go global, things get even more expensive. Regulations are different and patents – or some equivalent – have to be filed in all territories, with different maintenance and renewal requirements. You may find you're working with firms in China, Japan and the US, and having to track multiple patent scenarios.

An important factor in protecting your IP is budgeting for the future, perhaps to add more patents to your portfolio or to expand protection to new territories. Costs are most difficult to estimate when you start to consider how much you should budget for protecting your existing IP. If there's a likelihood of litigation, costs can depend very much on how easy it is to defend your position or to prosecute a company that you believe has infringed on your IP.

As always, it's about due diligence, and being an informed customer is key. Know what you need, know what your investors need, and pay the right amount of attention to selecting your IP support. Don't necessarily go with an attorney that someone running another business recommends – their business will not be the same or have the same needs as your business. Choose patent lawyers that have experience in the same space, and look for the experts, whether they are in a big firm or a sole trader.

Make sure you get advice from someone who understands business as well as how to patent intellectual property. You want the firm you appoint to have a strategic understanding of your business going forward, to help ensure that the advice they give is tailored to your needs and current status. Don't forget that things will change; will this attorney know what you might need next year, or in five years' time, and help you to prepare?

> The way we've identified areas of value and defensibility is by doing a very detailed intellectual property capture session with our IP attorneys to identify the areas of high value.
>
> Alex Schey, entrepreneur

From IP lawyer to IP entrepreneur – Zeev's story

Zeev Fisher was born and raised in Israel, attending law school and doing his military service in his capacity as a lawyer, defending military personnel who had contravened regulations.

When I finished my [military] duties, I rented a room in a firm of patent attorneys. They needed a litigator, which sounded great to me because I

*was always attracted to technology. I started doing their litigation work
and then got more and more involved on the strategy side. I found it
very interesting to sit down with really innovative people and see what
they were planning to do and how they were building new and exciting
products, how they were planning to launch them and how we could
make our contribution to that.*

Zeev Fisher, entrepreneur

Zeev then made a strategic decision to relocate and set up a UK
branch. He qualified as a solicitor and worked full-time as an IP lawyer
for around three and a half years, then left to set up his own company,
Pekama.

*Pekama started almost by accident. It started as me hiring developers
to build automation into how IP works and doing it for my own practice.
Then I met David Gill [Managing Director of St John's Innovation Centre
in Cambridge] and he got me excited. "Why don't you do something
more with that? If you need automation, surely more people need
automation. Why not set up a company?"*

The idea grew on Zeev for a while, and then he was introduced to a
potential investor who also saw great potential – not least because
he had been the client of an IP practice himself and knew how IP
portfolios could become opaque and hard to understand.

*Pekama started out building automation tools and a case management
tool to improve the work of IP attorneys. It evolved into what it is today:
a tracking, budgeting and portfolio management tool, primarily for IP
owners.*

Zeev notes the irony of the IP industry serving innovators and yet
being slow to innovate itself, and how Pekama can fill that gap.

*If a company builds a new piece of AI, or a new drug, or a new medical
device, it will always have patent attorneys and trademark attorneys all
around it. The most innovative companies in the world are surrounded by
IP attorneys. Those IP attorneys themselves deliver their core competence
– drafting patent applications and preparing trademark applications –
typically to a very high standard, but when it comes to innovation and
delivering exciting services, finding ways to deliver added value, creating*

clarity and transparency on the client side, there has been no change in the way that this profession conducts itself since, pretty much, forever. There has been a gradual movement to using less paper, but what we see in other sectors of the legal space – of more software and better client experience, better ways of delivering service – none of these things are happening in the IP space.

Zeev Fisher, entrepreneur

Intellectual property and exits

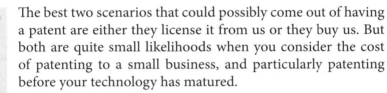

The best two scenarios that could possibly come out of having a patent are either they license it from us or they buy us. But both are quite small likelihoods when you consider the cost of patenting to a small business, and particularly patenting before your technology has matured.

Alex Schey, entrepreneur

An IP portfolio tends to make exits through acquisition easier for several reasons, including its impact on the competitive landscape and valuing the company overall.

You might be able to develop a robust patent and IP strategy by looking at the IP strategy of companies that are potential acquirers. By getting ahead of them – patenting in front of their direction of travel – you could put your company in the position of being an irritant to them, a roadblock that they need to open up. At that point, the acquiring company might need to access your patent portfolio to add to their own technology or to prevent it from being snapped up by a competitor. Cambridge gene sequencing company Solexa, for instance, was acquired by US company Illumina so that they could incorporate the technology in their sequencing machines, creating the breakthrough that brought the cost of gene sequencing down to affordable levels.

A patent portfolio can be easier to quantify than a brand or a service, and some acquirers value patents highly. One investor describes an exit where the majority of the value of a deep tech business was in its patent portfolio, with around ten patents costing the acquirer at least £50,000 each. In another exit, the patents were valued at around £1 million each.

The value was in the IP – Victor's story

Victor Christou's first company, Opsys, developed organic light-emitting diode (OLED) display technology. While the co-founders planned to go into production, at the outset they were focused on the technology itself. Because the product wasn't defined, they needed to keep all their options open.

> We filed as much IP as we could on the research, and we picked up as much IP as we could as well. So whenever IP became available, we bought it – because it's a very erratic journey growing your business, and you need to be spontaneous and agile and think quite broadly.
>
> Victor Christou, entrepreneur and investor

The team wanted to make sure they had all the ingredients they might need, and couldn't be sure which would be key.

> I think you need to be dogmatic in following your belief, but also opportunistic in trying to maximise opportunity and maximise possibilities for the business. We pivoted the business from one set of materials that we were researching to another set that we picked up from another research group at the University of Oxford, and put that technology into Opsys. It was rolling that IP into Opsys that proved to be the value driver in the business.

The Opsys policy of protecting as much as they could led them into a debate with another company in the space, Cambridge Display Technology. The discussion centred on the definition of a polymer.

> CDT were slightly ahead of us and they were always the bigger player, but we felt we had better technology secured through a differentiated IP portfolio. CDT's ambition was to consolidate IP in the OLED space, and because we had a clear point of differentiation protected by patents and know-how, it became obvious that the best way forward was to combine the businesses. As a result, CDT bought the patents and other assets of

Opsys and transferred the employees to CDT to capture the intangible IP and know-how.

The lesson for me as a founder was that we'd raised substantial capital to build a production line, but the true value-creation part of the business was the IP in the form of patents and employee knowledge.

Selling the IP, now found in all sorts of display applications including TVs and mobile phones, did not mean giving it up completely. Although they sold the production line, there were other options to explore.

We took a back-licence to the IP for non-display related technologies. We created a spin-in business, rather than a spin-out business, in a company called Arborescent, which is still going today and looking at sensors and detectors for things like explosives.

Victor Christou, entrepreneur and investor

THREE THINGS ABOUT INTELLECTUAL PROPERTY

- Some forms of IP can be protected by patents, trademarks, copyright, industrial design or utility models. Other forms of IP – such as processes, know-how or company culture – have to be protected in other ways.
- Sometimes it is better to keep something secret than to patent it and reveal it to the world.
- An intellectual property strategy will help you to decide what should be patented or protected in some other way, how much money will be needed to file and then protect any formal protection, and when it should be done.

CHAPTER 9

Cash flow

6 Revenue is vanity, profit is sanity – but cash is reality.

A t the time of writing, WeWork has just postponed its planned
IPO on the NASDAQ stock exchange. An investment manager quoted in the *Financial Times* commented that it was the first
time he'd seen a unicorn (a private company valued at $1 billion
or more) with 'zero support from either debt or equity investors'.
What happened? The company has a global footprint in its branded
co-working spaces, but – as the *Financial Times* also reported –
'the company lost roughly two dollars for every dollar of revenue

it generated in the first half of 2019'. Having been valued at $47 billion as recently as January 2019, the company was now looking at a valuation of $15 to 18 billion.

Another company trying to shore up its finances at the time of writing is global travel group Thomas Cook. The company is negotiating with potential funders and banks to refinance and secure the company's future, to the tune of some £1.1 billion. In the first half of 2019, the company recorded a loss of £1.5 billion.

Both of these companies may well succeed in sorting out their finances – they might even be deemed too big to fail – and presumably investors who do stick with them will hope that the businesses come out more streamlined and efficient on the other side. But, while the numbers might be different, their situation is repeated in businesses of all sizes.

An investment expert questioned about the Thomas Cook situation told the BBC that, 'Companies don't go out of business because they have too much debt. They go bust because they run out of cash.' At the time of proof-reading, some months later, Thomas Cook had indeed gone into liquidation, and WeWork was still under pressure.

Every business that fails runs out of cash. But running out of cash is not the cause of failure, it is a symptom of something going wrong. If a company is making a loss – because it has been unable to find a product–market fit or has some other systemic problem and can't see a way to solve it – eventually its investors and lenders will lose faith and cease supporting it. Small start-ups can be particularly vulnerable because they have yet to prove themselves, so convincing investors to stay on board might be harder. Even if a business is making a profit, the increasing demands of a rapidly expanding customer base can cause cash flow problems. Consequently, monitoring and controlling cash flow is part and parcel of start-up life.

What is cash flow?

Investopedia.com defines cash flow as 'the net amount of cash and cash-equivalents being transferred into and out of a business'. The definition goes on to say, 'At the most fundamental level, a company's ability to create value for shareholders is determined by its ability to generate positive cash flows, or more specifically, maximize long-term free cash flow.' 'Free' cash flow refers to the cash that is left (i.e. available for discretionary spending) once all other obligations are met.

If a company has positive cash flow, it can pay down debts, return money to shareholders, invest in assets and processes that will benefit the business, build a reserve for major expenditures in the future or to hedge against a possible downturn, and meet the payroll every month.

Unsurprisingly, if a company has negative cash flow, there are hard decisions to be made. Many entrepreneurs don't take a salary in the first one or two years of building their business because there simply isn't enough cash to pay them when all the other expenses of setting up and running a business are paid. Plenty of entrepreneurs stay in their day job for this reason, building their business in the evenings and weekends until they feel confident the business will be able to support them.

Time really *is* money

Time is money, as they say, and when you're trying to manage your cash flow, you have to take into account where and how you are spending your time. How much does it 'cost' your business if you are putting your time into things that are not core to your strategy? It can be very tempting to attend events aimed at entrepreneurs, or read yet another blog; but could those hours be used for generating cash rather than using it up?

> There is just so much 'noise' – your email, your LinkedIn notifications, your Facebook, Instagram, etc. You are constantly bombarded with information and I think as a founder it's even worse. You're thinking, do I need to be at that conference? Do I need to join that accelerator? Do I need to raise this money? So trying to filter out the noise and just focus on building what you're building is absolutely key.
>
> Chris Smith, investor

Elin Haf Davies learnt quickly how important time management was going to be – and how to take control of her time, rather than let it be controlled by others. 'Time really is your most precious asset,' she says. And protecting her time, as she described it, became increasingly important as she recognised its relationship to cash flow.

> I don't mean time as in, "It's going to take me three hours to write this investor deck, or eight hours to write these financial forecasts." It's more to do with time duration from start to finish, because by the time you send it to somebody, and then they read it, and then send it back, and then you have a meeting, and then they have to have another meeting...It's that combination of cashflow and time – that's where the biggest problems happen, because things don't ever work as quickly as you anticipate.
>
> Elin Haf Davies, entrepreneur

Another part of the time equation for you and your business is that, when you are launching an innovative product, you will probably be early to market. By definition, an innovative product is something the market hasn't seen before, so there will be a phase of educating and demonstrating the benefits before you begin to gain traction.

Because of this, another aspect of cashflow is to look at timing of product launch and when sales are likely to ramp up. Are you managing your cash in the expectation of lots of revenue from launch day? Or are you managing your cash with the expectation that sales will build slowly and you'll need to keep enough cash in the budget to get you through? Or will you need to raise another round of investment to keep you going? Take care not to get overly optimistic; make realistic plans for your business and realistic plans for your cash.

When you're early to market, you risk running out of 'runway'. That is, you don't have enough cash to get to the point of take-off, or positive cash flow. The longer the runway, the harder it is to manage your cash, and also the harder it is to stay focused on the vision and not lose faith.

> It's really hard to stay motivated and passionate about something for months and years when you're exhausted and have no cash.
>
> Elin Haf Davies, entrepreneur

Bootstrapping

Bootstrapping is a familiar term among entrepreneurs. Essentially, it means making do with what you've got. It is derived from the expression 'pulling yourself up by your own bootstraps', implying that you succeed by your own means, without any outside help. Taking no salary, eating a lot of lentils, using a bicycle rather than taking public transport – these are just a few of the sacrifices entrepreneurs make to get their businesses off the ground without going to external funders.

> We managed to persuade an awful lot of friends to come and do stuff for free. We were struggling for cash, but we managed to persuade people to write the code, we managed to persuade people to do marketing, for free.
>
> Andy Phillipps, entrepreneur and investor

Many investors like to see some evidence of bootstrapping before they'll invest, because it not only demonstrates how committed the entrepreneur is to their idea, but also that they'll most likely be equally careful with any cash invested. It also means that the entrepreneur is already working towards product–market fit.

> When people come into pitches for the first time and say, "We're going to build this," you ask, "What have you done so far?" If they reply, "We're waiting to raise the money before we actually go out and build it," that's a massive turnoff.
>
> If someone's building a marketplace, and they don't have any of the software but they're running a marketplace on Excel, email and phone calls, they're basically proving the model even if they haven't got the software yet. I like to see people who do a lot before they come to us and ask for funding.
>
> Chris Smith, investor

Bootstrapping is not always intentional. Sometimes there just aren't the investors around with the appetite to fund a start-up. Paul Forster and Rony Kahan founded an internet job platform for finance professionals after meeting at international business school INSEAD in the late 1990s. This was in the early days of the internet, and they were planning to seek outside funding. But their timing couldn't have been worse and, in the end, they were forced to bootstrap the new business. However, as Paul points out, this turned out to be a blessing in disguise.

> We hit the top of the dotcom bubble and were trying to raise funding right at the time when VCs had realised the writing was on the wall and things were going to come to a sticky end, which was good and bad. It was pretty tough to build a business with no outside funding. But on the positive side, we developed this kind of DNA of doing a lot with a little and bootstrapping the business. And I think that served us in good stead afterwards, having built a business during that very, very difficult time during 2000, 2001 and 2002.
>
> Paul Forster, entrepreneur and investor

Paul went on to found another company, and then into angel investing, and carried his experiences of bootstrapping through to how he views potential investee companies.

> If you can see that somebody has done a lot with a little, and has managed to stretch limited resources and is evidently cost-conscious, that's a very positive signal. And obviously the opposite – if you see somebody has raised a lot of funding in their previous business, burned through a lot of capital, and had very unhappy investors who felt like their money had gone down the drain and not been stewarded well – then that's a negative signal.
>
> Paul Forster, entrepreneur and investor

Andy Phillipps faced a similar situation when he launched ActiveHotels with business partner Adrian Critchlow, and also sees the benefits of being obliged to bootstrap.

> At that time the VC industry was collapsing and very, very few people wanted to invest. It helped that we had good operational advice on how to grow a business from cash flow, and as a result, we became profitable quite quickly.
>
> Andy Phillipps, entrepreneur and investor

Fire life protection company Plumis also found that raising funding would be a challenge in the early days, and the founders had to adapt to match their circumstances.

> We asked for too little. But I'm not sure we would have convinced anybody to put in more, so we got the amount we were able to get and tried to do the best with what we had. For many months, we didn't pay ourselves. We did all sorts of cost containment strategies so we could survive. I moved to a place where I would be fully subsidised; Yusuf moved to his parents' house. Our first office was in the HMS President, which was a World War 2 corvette located quite near Blackfriars on the river Thames. It took a while to get used to the fact that it was undulating as the Thames Hopper [a water taxi] went up and down the river, but it was affordable.
>
> Even today we are highly bootstrapped, but we've learned that that was the only way forward – especially in our slow-moving industry where new products are not adopted quickly.
>
> William Makant, entrepreneur

Bootstrapping can have unintended consequences, from not knowing how to spend money when you do secure investment, to putting your company in a better position than if it had had a large cash injection at the beginning.

> We'd bootstrapped for so long that, when we came to the actual moment where we could say, "Let's invest, let's grow the team," we resisted, because we weren't sure about what to spend. But it was a good time for investors to get us to change and grow, and invest more into R&D to be able to get the product launched.
>
> William Makant, entrepreneur

As William notes, the bootstrapping mind-set is different to that where funding is abundant. But he also sees now that his company has benefited from the constraints that bootstrapping imposed on the team.

> We knew nothing about the industry, so now we can clearly see that if we'd raised more money, we would have insisted on a path that, only now, seven years later, is showing any interest.
>
> If we'd had a lot more money, we'd have got more staff and fallen off a cliff long before the market had caught up with what we were presenting to them.
>
> Being bootstrapped meant we were able to pivot; we could change our focus much more quickly because there were only three of us and it took much less money, much less cost, to pivot.
>
> William Makant, entrepreneur

As with everything, though, there are counter-arguments. Some businesses, particularly in sectors like biotech, require significant funding from the outset and there simply is no way to bootstrap them.

There can also be situations where a market opportunity has to be seized before it's too late, and that, too, might require an injection of funds. So don't assume you have to bootstrap your business. Just make sure you understand how and when it might be the best option.

Bootstrapping and learning about your customers at the same time – Ronan's story

When Ronan Perceval founded his company Phorest, he intended to bootstrap from the start. His reasoning was that, without investors involved, any decisions made would put the business first rather than putting the investors first. As a result, the company didn't take any funding for the first seven years.

Phorest was originally founded to develop a software platform for any small business, and initially aimed at those that took clients on appointment – such as dentists, doctors and hairdressing salons – where the problem was loss of cash through no-shows. Phorest's early customers did, indeed, come from a variety of sectors, but the business was too broad and horizontal to start gaining traction in any of the sectors, and each sector needed its own set of features.

In order to keep bootstrapping the business, Ronan had to take a day job, and he made the crucial decision to go and work in one of the sectors that had already shown an interest in the Phorest product. He knew that they could only grow the business by going deeper into one sector.

> We were broke, so I needed money. I needed a job, and I could have gone and worked in a fast-food restaurant or something like that and worked on the business in the evening, but I decided to try out one of the industries and see which one might have potential. The idea was I would go to work in a dentist surgery, but I ended up getting a job in a salon and I ended up loving it.
>
> I was hitting two birds with one stone…and it was amazing. It opened my eyes to everything about how a salon works, about how hairdressers think, what's cool about the industry. You need to love an industry if you're going to spend your life in it, and I fell in love with the industry.
>
> Ronan Perceval, entrepreneur

One of the things that Ronan discovered was that, although salons tend to be small businesses, together they make up a huge industry sector.

> The salon industry is absolutely massive – it's bigger than all the other industries we were targeting. That's something that people don't realise.

You're looking at 60 million people working in salons as hairdressers or beauty therapists worldwide. On top of that, you're looking at another 40, 50 million people who work in businesses providing services or products for those salons. I think it's the seventh largest employer worldwide. So it's a huge industry in its own right, but it's not apparent because it's such a cottage industry — 95% of those salons are owner operated. It doesn't have the same presence on the high street or in people's consciousness of being a huge industry, but that means it's a massive opportunity.

Bootstrapping does mean that growth can be slow, but, as noted earlier, that might not turn out to be a negative thing, and Ronan sees how bootstrapping may have held the company back at times, but ultimately helped them to get to the right place.

We would have undoubtedly gone much faster if we'd raised money, because, when every cent counts, you can only take advantage of an opportunity when you can afford to. So you're saying no to lots of things that might have been a good idea, or you're not expanding fast when you're hitting a vein of opportunity.

The big positive is almost the same thing but in reverse. When you can only do certain things and you're so limited as to what you can try, you really think your options through and you don't just throw mud on the wall and hope it sticks. You really want to be sure when you're spending money that it's going to work. And as a result, you probably do say no to a lot of stuff that would have been distracting.

The end result, although they might not have anticipated it at the time, was to create a business that was not only built on secure foundations, but also had the luxury of not rushing to grab the first funding it could find.

We had to build a business that was self-sustaining, which meant that we were constantly in control of our destiny. We never had to go, "We've got to raise money now," and then raise it from somebody that maybe wasn't aligned with our values or had different expectations of what we were going to do with the business.

Ronan also found that another benefit of bootstrapping was how it helped to create a strong culture within the company.

Bootstrapping created a culture internally in Phorest that was incredibly cost-driven. Everybody minded the cents. I didn't have to worry about anybody in the organisation spending money when they shouldn't have because everyone was basically as tight as you can imagine. That was an amazing thing to build the organisation on, to have that trust between everyone so we know we're all going to look out for what the company is spending money on.

Few companies bootstrap to the point where they don't need any external funding, but what Phorest did with its cost-conscious culture was get to a position where they could pick and choose funders rather than simply take what was offered.

When we did finally raise money, we got to choose who we raised money from and made sure that we chose investors who were aligned with us. We could take our time because we were profitable – not massively profitable, but we weren't losing money – and that has led to a really good position now. Granted, it has taken us 15 years to get here, but the investors we do have don't own the majority of the business, so we still have majority control. And they don't have any strange terms in the agreement that would force us to sell their shares or anything. They're in it for the long haul as well…so it's worked out very well in the end.

Ronan Perceval, entrepreneur

Cash flow and customers

We've seen how working with customers can help put you in a better position to generate revenues, but that can bring its own cash flow issues.

Once you find your product–market fit, you'll have a customer base. Now, you need cash for other things, because those customers have to be supported in some way – perhaps with account management, bug-fixing or consultancy – and you'll already be working on new products, new recipes, upgrades, or wider applications for your technology, so your cash will need to flow in multiple directions.

❝ There is a tension between not having enough revenue and having too many customers placing too many demands on the business. You're always worrying about revenue on the one hand, but on the other hand you're worrying about all the different product features that your customers are crying out for. There's a fine line – haven't got enough customers, have too many customers – and you never seem quite able to get that balance right, so it's a bit of a rollercoaster.

Chris Mairs, entrepreneur and investor

The timings of cash in and cash out will become more critical as you manage the additional outlays.

If you get orders for lots of products, you need capital to produce those orders, particularly if you're in consumer products or something that requires something to be built and created. You have to keep a very close eye on the balance. You can get too many orders and kill the company because financing the materials and paying employees happens before the money comes in.

Joel Solomon, investor

Keeping an eye on cash flow

So how do you keep track of cash and make sure you don't get into a difficult situation? Obviously, a robust accounting system is key to knowing where your cash is coming in and going out. This is where you need to spend on getting the right advice. Paying for the level of financial expertise your company needs is money well spent. Even if you can read a balance sheet, you will have too many other tasks to give it your full attention constantly.

Be aware that you may face problems with late payments. The Asset Based Finance Association reported that small businesses in the UK have greater problems with late payments than large businesses. Their survey results showed that small companies wait 72 days on average for payment, and late payments were the main cause of cash flow problems. A simple but clear rolling cash flow forecast covering receipts and payments will help you keep on top of debts and hopefully spot potential late payments before they cause trouble.

Don't forget that cash equivalents are not cash: you cannot use them to pay salaries or suppliers. They may look nice on the balance sheet, but they won't help much when the payroll comes around.

Another thing that entrepreneurs often fail to grasp is the fact that high revenues don't necessarily mean high profits. If your cost of customer acquisition (CCA) – the total sum it takes to win each customer – is high, then the profit margin is likely to be low and you will need to keep that customer for a long time in order to get a decent return. This is what's known as the Customer Lifetime Value (CLV). Buyers who only buy once are expensive, and your cash flow forecasting needs to take this into account.

Finally, you, members of your board and your advisors should keep a watching brief on macroeconomic trends. Yes, you might be a small business with a narrow market to begin with, but external events may still have an impact. The investment landscape changes quickly in response to a crisis – such as the tech bubble bursting in the early 2000s – and also changes as different technologies or commodities go in and out of fashion. At present, AI and machine learning are getting the lion's share of tech venture capital, but it wasn't that long ago that telecoms were the flavour of the month – and once upon a time, it was railways. Things change, and you need to keep an eye on the big picture in order to be ready for – and perhaps take advantage of – a new direction. That could well require cash in the bank as well as cash from the hands of investors.

THREE THINGS ABOUT CASH FLOW

- Watch your cash flow carefully. Running out of cash can mean running out of road, and you can't pay salaries or suppliers with cash equivalents or ideas, so you need to get good advice and hire the best financial skills you can.
- High revenues don't necessarily mean high profit margins.
- Use all the means at your disposal to keep the cash flowing: reduce costs, increase profits, get better payment terms from your suppliers, chase customers for payment, and borrow.

CHAPTER 10

Scaling and pivoting

Scaling and pivoting are two things that you'll hear a lot about in the world of entrepreneurship. While there are certainly well-established definitions of scaling involving specific rates of growth, there are plenty of phases of the enterprise journey that feel like scaling – even if they don't quite fit official criteria. And sometimes, people will talk about pivots that, on closer inspection, turn out to be evolutions in the business model rather than revolutions. Is a pivot about a complete change in direction, a new product, a dramatically modified vision, or a completely different customer?

It's important not to get too hung up on the terminology. After all, you're growing a business and growing your customer base, and if your customer base develops in an unexpected direction, you'll have to scale, or pivot, or both, to stay with them.

Scaling

People talk about scaling all the time in the entrepreneurial and business world, but what exactly does it mean?

The influential 2014 Scale-Up Report, authored by Sherry Coutu, used the same definition of a scale-up as the OECD, Nesta and other governmental and non-governmental organisations:

> A 'scale-up' is an enterprise with average annualised growth in employees or turnover greater than 20 per cent per annum over a three-year period, and with more than 10 employees at the beginning of the observation period.

As the report states,

> The definition aims to identify companies which have experienced sustained company turnover (revenue) growth from customer orders, because this is the most reliable measure of whether customers are buying the company's products and services, and in turn this is a proxy for how innovative the company is.

Other definitions focus on metrics such as a specific turnover threshold, the number of users for products delivered online, or percentage of turnover sourced internationally. Generally, the idea is that, once the business model is proven and the product or service is starting to gain traction, the business should scale (i.e. grow) significantly. At this point, the task is no longer finding the product–market fit, but instead to sell more product and get operations right to cope with increased demand.

But you might feel that you're 'scaling' when you go from two or three founders taking no salary to a team of seven or eight employees: you've more than doubled in size already. That, too, is rapid growth and can create major change.

Growing the team can be a key part of reaching your next investment point on the journey, so it can be expensive, and may have to happen very quickly before you run out of cash. CMR Surgical, under CEO Martin Frost, went from 4 employees to around 40 people in the space of 18 months. They knew that they would need a prototype product to demonstrate to potential Series

B investors, and knew that it could not be delivered by a handful of people.

So even though you're just in the start-up phase and recognise that you have plenty of mountains to climb, you perhaps need to keep an eye on how the business could grow in the future and think about how scaling might affect your core business.

The "oh, ****" moment – Pilgrim's story

The biggest surprise in the AlertMe journey, which was nine years end to end, was that I had originally thought of it primarily as a development challenge. We knew we would have to develop a lot of hardware and software, develop the proposition and so on, and I thought once we got over that big hump – which would take a lot of time and money – then we could just scale.

Pilgrim Beart, entrepreneur

What surprised Pilgrim was that scaling meant having to do things he hadn't anticipated having to do, and adapting the business model. Once they had found their product–market fit and begun to build a supply chain so they could outsource non-core activities, such as manufacturing components (as described elsewhere), what they needed to do for their customers changed. AlertMe became a service provider, which brought its own set of challenges.

I thought of scaling as just something that would sort of happen. But as we got over the product-development hump and we started scaling, we discovered that – surprise, surprise – when you have a connected product, it becomes a service. You are a service provider, and the product is just a way to deliver the service. And if you're a service provider, then the day-to-day challenge is whether you're doing a good job of delivering that service. Are your devices all working? Your operations team, your customer support team, will all be focused on that challenge. That's what your money will be spent on, that's where your attention will go.

That was when we realised that we had migrated from R&D into operations and now the game was scaling, and that we hadn't invested nearly enough in the tools we would need to help us do operations well.

As Pilgrim and the AlertMe team found, the growth they were experiencing changed their costs and where they needed to focus resources.

> *This doesn't happen overnight. It's a transition from R&D to operations. Operating costs grow in tandem with the number of devices, and it's very easy with a connected product to end up in a situation where, as your number of customers grows, so do your losses. You can end up in a situation where you're doing far too much manually. People are expensive, and therefore as the number of devices grows, you end up making a bigger and bigger loss. It's quite hard to dig yourself out of that hole, but it happened to us in about 2010 at AlertMe, and because you've asked me not to swear, I won't tell you exactly what we called this moment, but it's the "oh something" moment.*
>
> *You start to confront the true economics of your business at scale: how much money you make per month per customer – your MRR [monthly recurring revenue] – and how much you're spending per month per customer, and whether one is bigger than the other.*

Pilgrim also discovered that scaling wasn't just about the finances.

> *It's also about whether you're delivering a good experience to your customers. If you've got a 1% problem, and you've got a hundred customers – well, it's just one slightly weird customer. Who knows whether that's a hardware problem, or a software problem? But if you've got a million customers and you've got a 1% problem, that's a front-page news problem. And so, as you grow, your quality needs to get much, much better.*
>
> *Which means not only your hardware and software has to get better, but your processes must get better, too. Devices will go wrong in lots of different ways. They are being deployed into the real world, which is an uncontrolled place, so that's just inevitable; and so, your processes for dealing with things that are not working and getting them working again become critical.*

What the AlertMe team were experiencing was not new – in fact, subsequently they found that many other businesses had gone through the same challenges – but they simply hadn't expected such a radical impact on the business they originally thought they were building.

Towards the end of my time at AlertMe, I went and talked to lots and lots of other companies that were doing connected products, in all sorts of other markets – so not just connected home, but smart city, medical, connected office, you name it – and we got the same two reactions again and again.

The first was that people who hadn't scaled just didn't get it, they didn't understand that this would happen. And the other was, [among] the few that had scaled, there was lots of eye rolling and recognition of the fact that, yes, as you start to get to scale, then day-to-day operations become the challenge.

Anticipating and planning for a possible future is never easy, and it takes time away from all the other challenges of starting an entrepreneurial business, but it could be critical to your business.

Along with his start-up journeys in the UK, Pilgrim has spent some time in Silicon Valley, and believes that finding a start-up's core excellence and divesting non-core elements is something more hard-wired into the entrepreneurs there, which helps them to scale more efficiently.

I think if you do something again and again, you start to learn patterns. You start to see patterns that are not unique to the start-up or as a result of luck. They're systemic things… There's a massive opportunity for you to grow as the market grows, but what are the dynamics of that?

You're not trying to invent the whole thing from scratch. A big problem with inventing everything from scratch – apart from all the money and time it takes – is that, when you're finished, your thing will not work with anyone else's and you won't be able to ride off anyone else's scaling curve.

It's very important to understand when that's happening in your market, and to proactively divest yourself of all the bits that you had to do for practical reasons but which are not really core to your excellence.

Pilgrim Beart, entrepreneur

When you have to scale to realise your vision – Toby's story

Another company that is embarking on the scale-up adventure is Simprints. But as a social enterprise aiming to create a step-change in health and levels of poverty in the poorest communities, the direction of growth and problems are somewhat different.

> *What growth means in concrete terms is actually transitioning from the pilot phase to our first scale projects. We're now in 10 different deployments all across Sub-Saharan Africa and South Asia, and we're about to start our first national-scale deployment in Bangladesh with BRAC. This is going to be a massive challenge. We've never taken on a project of this size or scope before. I know we've got a lot of learnings coming down the pipeline, but it is also incredibly exciting, because if we can make this work, we can prove that you can deploy biometrics accurately, safely, robustly and cost effectively at national scale to improve the way that we fight disease and fight poverty at the front lines.*
>
> Toby Norman, entrepreneur

Toby recognises that their challenges include building the evidence base to demonstrate that what they are trying to do is viable.

> *In order to support that work, we're also going to need to very clearly build an evidence base that shows that this is physically changing people's lives. A big part of our commitment is actually research. It's doing things, for example, like randomised control trials, impact evaluations and other hard quantitative evaluations of the actual difference using something like a fingerprint, for example, makes to improving maternal healthcare coverage, or decreasing fraud in cash transfers, or trying to fight teacher absenteeism in Sub-Saharan Africa. Can we show that those things have a concrete impact in people's lives?*

For Simprints, scale is also about impact on society rather than on the bottom line.

> *Even if we achieve massive scale, if what Simprints is bringing to the table isn't adding value to individual humans, there's no point to the*

*work we do. And that's why I think you really need to have both — what
we call at Simprints the impact equation, that combination of breadth
of scale with…depth of impact and actual difference to a person. And
if you can achieve both of those things, then I think you're really onto
something.*

Toby Norman, entrepreneur

The pivot

> The thing you think you're going to do and the thing that you
> will do are two different things.
>
> Jon Bradford, entrepreneur and investor

Along with scaling, there's a lot of talk about the pivot. In *The
Invested Investor*, we told the story of William Tunstall-Pedoe and
his company True Knowledge, which was eventually acquired by
Amazon. The company went through a series of pivots where they
took their core vision – 'to answer any question in any language in
one second or less' – and went through several ways of delivering
that goal until they hit the sweet spot: voice.

Each time the company pivoted, it changed its product, although
the underlying idea remained the same. The first attempt to mon-
etise the technology was a website that answered questions (competing with Google when that was still a sensible option). Then the
company adopted a licensing model, offering its technology to larger
search companies, however that proved a hard sell. The third itera-
tion used a version of search engine optimisation to direct traffic to
the company's new website, trueknowledge.com. This model gained
traction and the company started to grow. But then Google, by now
recognisable as the giant it is today, changed its algorithm and True
Knowledge was in trouble. A final change – 'betting the company',
as William has described it – led to the release of a voice assistant for
mobile phones, called Evi. One download every ten seconds since
launch, Evi became not only the name of the product but also the
name of the company. Today, Evi is better known as Alexa.

> The pivot. I hate that word.
>
> Jon Bradford, entrepreneur and investor

Investor Jon Bradford sees the so-called pivot as more of an evolution of the business model.

> Product–market fit is not a single point in time…As the product changes and as you evolve, as you get larger, your customer base is going to change. And as your customer base changes, actually your product is probably going to have to change – or your services – at the same time.
>
> So it's something you constantly have to be aware of and be evolving and changing depending upon your customer group. Some have done that incredibly well and some have failed because they initially fix the problem for a small demographic. But when they move on to the bigger demographic, they fail to change; they just don't grow.
>
> Jon Bradford, entrepreneur and investor

Is it a pivot? – Ofri's story

Ofri Ben-Porat's company, Pixoneye (now Edgify), started with the idea of developing a new Data Management Platform to help brands personalise how they interact with their customers more accurately. He saw that the available offerings were poor – results for gender, for instance, may be only 50% accurate – and so could cause brands more problems than they solved. There were also issues around where and how the data were handled.

> *We wanted to create a holistic place where the brand owns the data, analyses the data and engages with the data completely on the device.*
>
> Ofri Ben-Porat, entrepreneur

The way Ofri's company delivers on that promise has changed for internal and external reasons. Technological change, especially the increasing sophistication of the smartphone, has been part of that process.

The idea is still the same. The way that we create this engagement and interact with the user is different. Four years ago, we were going to look at people's personal photo galleries on their phones. Today, we do an array of analysis. In those days, we dragged some things to the Cloud for deeper analysis, today we do everything on the device.

As well as technological change, the regulatory environment has become more complex since the company was founded, which prompted another swerve.

GDPR came along and we fully complied by pushing everything away from the Cloud onto the device. Our big IP is being able to use the device's CPU and GPU computing powers to run AI deep learning processes that would take a tonne of space.

Ofri believes that the reasons behind his start-up remain valid: they are still solving the problems they set out to solve. Their growth has been a question of responding to circumstances rather than making any major changes in direction.

It's very similar to where we started. There have been ups and downs, but I wouldn't call them pivots because the idea is still the same, the vision is still the same. But we've definitely had challenges, like GDPR coming in, and brands not fully ready to analyse data or not fully ready to give up a Data Management Platform because of legacy.

Ofri Ben-Porat, entrepreneur

When customers don't want your product yet – Luke's story

Investor Luke Hakes has seen an interesting situation develop where a business had a good product that potential customers liked but weren't ready to buy until their current equipment became obsolete. The company needed to find a way to survive until the customers' purchasing cycles came around.

We invested in a cloud video production business, which was trying to move video production from on-premise to the cloud – a perfectly sensible idea. In five years' time, that's probably how all video production will be done. What we failed to appreciate, or underestimated, was the investment the customers had already made in equipment that was sitting in rooms on their premises. Whilst they loved the idea of cloud video production, they had also spent a million dollars on on-premise video production. Their argument was, "If you come back in three to five years, we'll buy your stuff. We have stuff that works now, and we don't see any reason to change it."

Luke Hakes, investor

The question for the entrepreneurs became whether they should continue trying to sell their solution, which everyone said would become popular in the next five years, or should they try to find a way to address a separate market with their technology? Given that the chances of having enough funding to survive until the market picked up were slim, the company had to try something new.

What happened was, the business pivoted into an industry sector that needed cloud video access and production capability today. That industry hadn't got a solution, and that made it a much more interesting offering.

A pivot could be the only way to avoid failure, but it wasn't going to be easy. The company was thinking about making a bold move into an industry they didn't know or understand, and that was daunting. All of a sudden, they had a lot of new questions to answer.

It was an industry that the CEO had no domain expertise or knowledge of, so they were very, very nervous about going in that direction. It was only by adding people around the CEO — and by the CEO finding others to work with — that they were able to get comfortable and confident about how they should go about addressing that market. How big was it? How did the players within that market operate? What would their requirements be? I think it will go on to be a very successful company. Had it stayed on the trajectory of wanting to work with video production companies, it would have failed outright.

Luke Hakes, investor

Pivoting to tick the right box – the Plumis story

Nothing we originally planned is in the current company. Not even the product. Not even the people.

William Makant, entrepreneur

William Makant and Yusuf Muhammad, co-founders of Plumis, say they went through several pivots. These pivots were driven by the search for product–market fit and the need for a major redevelopment of their original technology.

Our first product was a series of spray nozzles – water mist nozzles – that fitted underneath the kitchen tap. Basically, that allows you to retrofit a sprinkler system to protect a kitchen very, very easily.

Yusuf Muhammad, entrepreneur

The team thought that the initial customers for their fire protection device would be homeowners wanting to add an extra safety feature to their house, and housing associations looking to improve safety for their tenants. But despite plenty of media attention, nobody was buying.

We were attempting to validate the housing associations – which would mean large volumes but slower purchase cycles – and the consumer side. There were lots of consumers saying, "I'm interested," but none of these were converting to sales at all. And the housing associations showed lots of interest, too, but had no budget.

William Makant, entrepreneur

If they didn't find a way to sell their product, they weren't going to survive. Somehow, they had to find the right direction.

What we didn't understand when we first started is the driver for the fire safety industry – and it's regulation, plain and simple. It's a "grudge" purchase so you can tick a box, and we only got traction when we found a niche where we enabled someone to tick a box.

Yusuf Muhammad, entrepreneur

The niche came in the form of the UK's Building Regulations, which apply to homeowners renovating or converting their homes, and architects and builders constructing or extending buildings. Building control (as it is more commonly known) lists specific conditions and requirements that various categories of building work must comply with.

> *We had consumers knocking at our door saying, "I have building control telling me I have to put in sprinklers, and I'm wondering if I can put your tap spray system in my kitchen and my living room." We thought, "How on earth are we going to put a sink in the middle of their living room?" And we didn't even know what building control was!*
>
> William Makant, entrepreneur

All of a sudden, the Plumis team had to learn about the building codes and regulations and how their product could become part of the solution.

> *We went to a local building control office, learned exactly what they did and how our product could fit. They said, "Your product could be used for this very niche-specific loft conversion application, which is written into the guidance of the building regulations in the UK."*
>
> William Makant, entrepreneur

The pivot was to adapt the technology from being a sink attachment to something that could be installed anywhere. Traditional sprinkler systems have high water requirements and are laborious to install, and even harder to retrofit into existing buildings. The Plumis team came up with a system that not only used less water and was easy to install, but also detected the location of a fire and directed the water towards the source of the flames – as opposed to sprinkler systems that simply drenched the entire room. Now they had to meet a set of standards for sprinkler systems in order to be certified and approved as compliant with building control.

> *We had to adapt to this much slower and much higher barrier to entry of having to fire test – having to have third party scrutiny into everything we did with our product.*
>
> William Makant, entrepreneur

The new direction also meant a new route to market. They had to pivot the sales strategy.

> *The route to market is through installers, not direct to consumer. Once we had identified this niche — that we could help people to get their homes signed off and enable them to have more open plan, more desirable layouts — we had to educate the market that we were here, we were an easy solution. So we did a lot of presentations — to industry, to approvers, to architects so they would specify us, and to installers.*

> Yusuf Muhammad, entrepreneur

Plumis was founded in 2008, and the first installation of the new product was around three years later.

> *You will find out that what you originally planned — your product and your company — will change very rapidly, and you just have to be ready to change.*

> William Makant, entrepreneur

THREE THINGS ABOUT SCALING AND PIVOTS

- Scaling will introduce problems that you won't have thought of while developing your product, such as what follow-up support customers will need and what to do if you find you're now selling a service rather than a product.
- Pivots may be more about evolving the business model than about changing the direction of the business completely.
- You might need to pivot into a different market while your main target market matures.

CHAPTER 11

The End of the Adventure

How does the adventure end? The company might simply close down when the investors and senior leaders recognise that it is never going to succeed. Or it might fail by running out of cash and be forced to close, even if the team still believe in the vision. For the founder, the journey might end when, for whatever reason, they decide to step aside. There are probably, as Paul Simon didn't sing, 50 ways to leave a business.

In the sun-lit uplands of entrepreneurship, the adventure ends with a glorious exit: a huge sale to a mega-brand, or an IPO that takes the stock exchange by storm. The company goes on to become a household name around the globe, loved by all. The founders buy a fast car, a yacht and an island, and spend their days on the beach.

That is, of course, fantasy for most entrepreneurs. A different story is far more realistic. Yes, the company is acquired, but when all the cash is shared out, the sums might not be that big. The company can fall victim to circumstances outside its control – a financial crisis, say, or a natural disaster – or it can fall victim to its own problems.

Sometimes, the adventure ends because the founders want it to. Sometimes, it ends because it has to.

Taking the tough decision to close

> One of the things I've noticed – particularly in the mentoring work I do with entrepreneurs – is that it is often very, very, very difficult to decide that the business is not viable and you need to close it down. People are so emotionally invested in their business and have committed so much personally and financially that they are hanging on to see if they can just get some traction. They have a sense that, if we just do this, something will happen. If we pivot, something will happen. They've invested so much, the decision to quit is extremely difficult.
>
> Bridget Connell, investor

Why might the company close? Perhaps because the proposition isn't robust enough: the problem the entrepreneur thought they were solving is only felt by a small market. Perhaps because the next round of investment is not going to arrive after all and they can't keep hanging on any longer. Sometimes, when it comes down to it, the entrepreneur needs to be given permission to stop.

> If you are extremely driven and driving your own business, you won't give yourself that permission. You need someone

else to say, "It's okay to take some time out," or, "Based on my experience of having invested in x businesses, I don't think this is viable." It's not the same as telling them to do it, but sharing insight.

Bridget Connell, investor

Why companies fail

For investor Luke Hakes, there are three main reasons why companies fail: the people, the market and the money.

Number one is people, and that drives failure around a whole bunch of different vectors. The second is making something nobody really wants – essentially no product–market fit or just not solving a problem that's interesting. Third is running out of cash. That can happen for a bunch of reasons. Maybe you didn't have product–market fit and it took longer so you ran out of cash. Maybe you had to change the team and you hired the wrong people and ran out of cash. But ultimately, running out of cash is what caused failure.

Luke Hakes, investor

The people problem is a common issue, and there are several facets to it.

In some cases, it's hiring the wrong people. In some cases, it's the right people falling out with each other – disagreements between founders or early team members – or just failing to hire the right person into the right role, or failure to move people on quickly enough once you've realised they're the wrong person. Having the wrong people essentially prevents you from doing the right things in a whole host of areas. If you've got the wrong people in technology development, you build bad product. If you have the wrong people in marketing or no people in marketing, you don't market. If you have the wrong people in finance, maybe you have no financial controls and you waste money, or lose money in other ways.

> When you look down at all the reasons for failure, they come back to the team. If you were to invest in a team with the best ideas in the world and the ability to execute better than anybody else, you will have a successful company.
>
> Luke Hakes, investor

Another investor, Jessica Dick, agrees that these factors lie behind the failures she has seen, although there is also an element of timing, particularly for technology companies.

> The reasons for the failures varied quite widely. A couple of them got to market too late, or by the time they'd done enough work on the technology, some bigger players had taken over and it was just too late. Other reasons included the funding running out and being unable to secure further funding.
>
> Jessica Dick, entrepreneur and investor

Failing to secure follow-on funding can happen for a number of reasons. It might be that the company hasn't commercialised quickly enough, and investors can't see any real proof of product–market fit.

> You can do everything right, and if it's just the wrong timing – the market is not ready for it – even if you've done everything right, you haven't put a foot wrong, you're still going to be screwed.
>
> Dominic Hill, entrepreneur

It might be that the earlier investors decide not to, or are unable to, follow on, and this sends a negative signal to other potential investors. Making the decision to follow on or not is tricky when the company hasn't yet found the ingredients for growth.

> We've had an interesting time in the last couple of years where we've had to make that decision, "How much do we follow on in companies that we invested in at an early stage?" You can't

> follow on in all of them. You want to back the winners, but at the same time you get attached to the entrepreneurs, you want to support them. You always think there might be a way through.
>
> Jessica Dick, entrepreneur and investor

You could argue that, underneath all these, it yet again comes down to the people. Have you got the right team in place? Has the team been able to create the right answer to a real problem? Can you sell their answer into a large enough market? We've talked about the team before, and the importance of finding the right complementary skills. Building such a team is not something anyone can do, but it makes a big difference to your chances of success.

> If I could have one attribute that I could test for prior to making an investment, it would be the entrepreneur's ability to hire and retain talent. If an entrepreneur has that ability, almost certainly they will find a solution to the problem they face by finding somebody to find that solution.
>
> Luke Hakes, investor

Stepping aside, stepping down

> Just because you're a founder, doesn't mean you have to be the CEO.
>
> Emily Mackay, entrepreneur

Your journey might end when you step away from the company you founded. Reasons for doing this can range from feeling that your skills and experience are not what the company needs going forward, to burn-out – with plenty of alternatives in between.

As a company starts to scale, it is often time for new skills to be brought in, and this may well have to start at the top. There are numerous cases where founders have been perfectly good CEOs while the company has been finding its feet and beginning to gain traction, but they do not have the different skillset needed to run a rapidly growing and expanding company.

Sometimes, it's not so much about the skills as about what the individuals want to do next. Serial entrepreneurs in particular are keen to move on to the next project once they can see their company is up and running. They take the decision to continue playing to their own strengths – of creating something and getting it off the ground – rather than continue into the perhaps more predictable corporate domain.

At some point, as founder, you will have to be able to step outside yourself and make the right choice for the company – something which you may find hard to do. But if you have always been honest about your skills and motivations, and clear about what you can and cannot do – or are not willing to do – then you can make an informed and sensible decision about your next move.

Remember that stepping aside does not necessarily mean stepping out. Founders often find themselves making their best contribution in a different position to that of CEO. That, too, is something to keep in mind as the company grows: where are you best placed to utilise your skills for the benefit of the company?

Making sure you're the right person in the right place – Dominic's story

You've got to be able to think of yourself as a shareholder first and as a founder second.

Dominic Hill, entrepreneur

The people problem emerges in different ways, and one of them is in how the founders and key individuals assess their own skills and abilities. Are they honest with themselves about what they are capable of and whether they can deliver what the company needs? Dominic Hill has a realistic point of view.

I've never scaled a billion-dollar software company, but I have ambitions to. Am I the right person to be the CEO of that company? I'm not sure. If there's somebody better for the company, then as a shareholder, my interest is to put them in that position. And you need to think like that as a founder. First, you're a shareholder. Second, you're a founder. And if you think like that, then you'll always be aligned with your board, and you'll always be a reasonable person to talk to, and you'll always be on the right side of the decision. If you start thinking that somehow you're distinct from your shareholders, you're in dangerous territory.

Stepping aside as CEO would not necessarily mean stepping aside from the company. Dominic is clear about his ambitions and plans to tie any decisions about his role to his overarching vision for the company.

If I'm no longer CEO, I'm going to be product manager. I'm definitely in the company. I get out of bed in the morning because I want to change this industry, and I want to see the look in the eyes of all the people who told me that it couldn't be done or that it was a waste of time. I want to see that moment when they realise that they were wrong. Maybe that's arrogant and I'm hell-bent on it, but it's why I get out of bed. So I'm not going anywhere. And, in fact, I would say that it's the depth of that drive that would lead me to appoint somebody else CEO, because I'm so married to a positive outcome that even my own ego will be sacrificed in the pursuit of that positive outcome, that I'm secondary to that.

Dominic Hill, entrepreneur

Not all founders are CEO material – Emily's story

Emily Mackay's start-up journey has taught her where her strengths lie and how she can best use her skills to serve the company.

There is a sort of pattern, and I'm not quite sure where it's come from, but there is a pattern that if you come up with an idea for a company and you start it all off, you badge yourself CEO. Actually, the skills of a CEO are very particular and you may be a brilliant technical lead. You may be a brilliant scientist. You may be the creative brain behind something. Those skills may be extremely valuable to the company, but not as the CEO.

Emily Mackay, entrepreneur

Emily understands that now, but when she started her company, becoming CEO was the logical – and, indeed, only – step.

I made myself the CEO and got started because I was the only person executing. But a good skill set for a CEO is somebody who can tell stories and be the public face and be quite evangelistic about their mission and their vision, and that side didn't sit so comfortably with me.

I'm much more of an organiser. I'm good with the paperwork. I'm good at making sure that all the shareholders have the right bits of information that they need and everything is signed and dotted and watertight. But if I have to stand on stage and evangelise, that takes me outside my comfort zone.

There are plenty of alternatives to being CEO, and these roles can be combined with being a co-founder.

If I was to do this all again, I wouldn't necessarily badge myself CEO. Badge yourself founder. Give yourself that status, that's cool, but you can be a founder and something else. You can be the founder operating officer or finance director or whatever your skill set is.

As Emily points out, it's hard to think like this in the very early days because the title CEO so often goes to one of the founders, but looking ahead through the business plan could give you an idea of when things will need to change.

Being founder CEO can create challenges as the company grows. At some point, your passion will not be enough because you need certain professional skills to take the company to the next stage. I've seen it elsewhere. It can create friction because the founder CEO wants to retain that title. They feel like they've earned it by virtue of their input into the company and all the energy and sleepless nights they've had, but actually you need to be aware that you don't have to do that.

You can still be the founder, you can still have your shares, you can still have your exit – but have a different role.

Changing roles as the company grows is something that should be discussed early. It is far better to have an understanding in place from the start that changes will be needed, rather than to try and introduce the subject later when the founders may already feel entrenched in their roles.

I don't think that conversation happens with investors. I think it gets sort of glossed over until the point where you realise, "We need somebody who can really go and pitch to this kind of company and can close this kind of deal and so-and-so's not really that. What do we do about it?"

Better to have a plan between the founders and the investors that gives the founder a career path and a sense of progression and the status and so on that they want, but recognises their skills, or says, "Okay, to be the CEO of a Series B company, you're going to need to do this."

That gives the company options. The founder CEO may be willing to develop themselves and continue to lead, or they may decide it is time to focus on their existing skillset.

How do we put that training, those skills, that coaching in place so that you can say, "Do you want to do that? Do you want to be the person who goes on the Chinese trade missions? Or would you be happy if somebody else did that while you continue developing the software?"

Emily has seen this situation clearly herself, but doesn't feel that investors and founders are having those sorts of discussions on a regular basis, and that is a mistake.

I'd really encourage those conversations to happen. I don't think they are at the moment. Certainly I didn't witness or have it myself, but I think it would be a really healthy thing, and also give a sense that everyone's on the same page with how things are going to unfold, rather than it getting squeezed into a corner and then having to make some kind of decision.

Emily Mackay, entrepreneur

How do investors feel about changing CEO?

I warn my CEOs at the beginning they need to grow with the business – or faster than the business grows – in terms of their ability. Otherwise, they may not be CEO on exit. If you start early, then at least they'll work on that journey to try and always be slightly ahead, but they can't guarantee to do that.

Peter Cowley, entrepreneur and investor

Investors back not only the founder, but also the business. So if they feel that the founder is not in the right position, they may well intervene.

> Whilst being sympathetic to the founder, we've got to find the right role for them. If the founder is constraining the business, we need to remove that constraint or repurpose it. I think, in early-stage businesses, it's often terminal if you just fire a founder. It's never a good thing.
>
> Victor Christou, entrepreneur and investor

As Victor Christou points out, this is a very difficult situation, as the implications for morale in the business are complex. Some might be happy to see the founder move to a different position, others might be happier if they left altogether.

> We backed a business on an idea from the founder. The business is still going today and they've built a pilot plant in the US, but the founder stepped down from being chief executive to being the chief scientific officer and eventually left.
>
> Victor Christou, entrepreneur and investor

Ultimately, the goal is the good of the business, and all involved have to keep that as the basis for decisions.

> The founder is the person who has the vision. What you try to do is match their skillset with the skillset of business building. That's a difficult conversation, but it's one that we have all too often.
>
> Victor Christou, entrepreneur and investor

Reaching the exit

There are many players involved in an exit: the founders, the investors, the employees, the acquirers and, of course, the service providers who deal with the nuts and bolts of the process itself. Among the investors, there may be some who are no longer willing or able to follow on and are keen to get a return, while other investors might see better returns further down the line and want to stay on the journey. An exit will only work well if everyone is aligned.

Then there are different types of exit, which can impact on how easy it is to align everyone involved. Mergers and acquisitions (M&A) are the principal format. Others include later-stage funds, which buy out earlier investors; and initial public offerings (IPOs), which can be highly successful if you get the timing right, but sometimes prove difficult to pull off if the private equity market is falling out of love with your particular sector.

According to VC Max Bautin, M&As continue to be a strong source of potential exits.

> For the last 10 years, M&A was essentially the only realistic exit route, and these days there are a lot more corporates that are acquisitive. The multiples are higher. There are better choices. There are better ways of playing one corporate acquirer against another, which is always something that companies should try and engineer because corporates try to avoid that situation... and they use all sorts of clever tricks to do so.
>
> Max Bautin, investor

Later-stage funds, or secondary purchasers, have come back into the spotlight as investor behaviour changes.

> The secondary purchasers that were unheard of for many years are now back, and they're back at strength. We have seen offers for our companies, not even for 100% but sometimes 30, 40, 50, or 60% – a capital replacement offer from essentially private equity growth firms. They are prepared to pay multiples which are very close to what the strategists would pay. That, of course, often creates a great opportunity for the earlier-stage investors to exit prior to the master exit, which might take many more years to achieve.
>
> Max Bautin, investor

Again, it's all about the timing. Secondary purchasers are not necessarily buying themselves a guaranteed win, and the founders and earlier investors might reap the rewards.

> Even at later stages, there are still ongoing risks with a company. Sometimes, taking that early exit is not a bad thing, especially if you can take it at a price which is demonstrably comparable to what you would get if you were selling the whole business outright.
>
> Max Bautin, investor

Listing your company on a stock exchange can raise considerable amounts of money, but public listings are susceptible to a host of factors. Sometimes there is simply no appetite for investors to buy into an IPO. There is also the question of which stock exchange you should list on. Some UK companies purposefully listed on NASDAQ in New York to give them access to US investors and their often-deeper pockets, while others prefer to opt for smaller exchanges, like the Alternative Investment Market (AIM) in London, or NASDAQ First North in Sweden.

There are also alternative share-selling platforms being established – such as Funderbeam, where private investments can be traded.

> Businesses like Funderbeam are only starting to pick up, but the opportunity for liquidity prior to the actual exit – where they help shareholders exchange, sell and buy shares in exactly the same way that stock exchanges would – is also increasingly relevant. Hopefully, it will help earlier-stage investors to recycle their capital quicker, which ultimately will mean that we'll be able to back more businesses.
>
> Max Bautin, investor

This new option is uncharted water, so naturally 'buyer beware' is the order of the day.

❝ While people sometimes argue and ask whether the prices are a bit too high, I am not sure they are. A lot of these businesses are generating numbers which fully justify the numbers that they achieve. Some don't. There will always be speculation. There will always be irrational exuberance in this market. It's part of it, and it will swing from too positive to too negative every now and then. Again, that's part of the technology development cycle. But overall, I think we're in a very strong place, and I expect a lot of great things from the tech sector.

Max Bautin, investor

The whole process took about a year – Pilgrim's story

There's always this question about when to exit, and sometimes that will come from the investors because their fund's reaching the end of its life or whatever it is. And that's often not a very helpful dynamic. In our case, that wasn't the case as the investors were up for funding it further. So it was really a decision about what was the best roll of the dice.

Pilgrim Beart, entrepreneur

For Pilgrim and his team at AlertMe, one of the considerations was how the market was developing. Another was whether they were up for another challenge when bigger players were moving into the space.

The market was changing quite fast. Players like Nest, who had come into the market, were, counterintuitively, a good thing for us. Big competitors can be a great help, since they can create and establish value. A lot was happening, but I think we felt like we'd probably done enough rolls of the dice. It was time to find a home for AlertMe, especially as a large number of players were emerging who also wanted this kind of technology. British Gas was one of them, but there were plenty of others, so it felt like there was now a market for the company where there hadn't been one previously.

British Gas were already an investor in AlertMe, so they might have had an edge over other possible purchasers, but bringing in a corporate financier to oversee the process meant that the best outcome could be achieved, regardless of the apparent advantage for British Gas.

The whole process took about a year from the decision to actually selling the company. There was a bidding process, and in terms of the original investment terms we had to be careful that British Gas didn't end up having to sit on both sides of the deal. So they sometimes had to recuse themselves from discussions. That's a little bit delicate. It's both a help and a hindrance having an incumbent like that in place. We knew there probably was a customer for the company, but on the other hand, British Gas were by then our biggest customer for the product, so that's an interesting dynamic.

Finally, when all the options were on the table, the outcome became clear and AlertMe became part of British Gas.

It was a financial decision, at the end of the day, for the investors.

Pilgrim Beart, entrepreneur

Be prepared – David's story

David Cleevely sold his telecoms consultancy, Analysys, in 2004; but had he sold a few years earlier, the price would have been much higher. When he turned down the first offer in 2000, the sector was booming and it seemed like the company would be even more valuable in a few years' time. Then the dotcom bubble burst, and the fall-out lasted for four, stressful years.

We were the last people standing because everybody else got swept away, which enabled us to survive and finally sell up to the company who had offered a lot more money in 2000.

David Cleevely, entrepreneur and investor

One of the lessons for David was to be prepared. The company had around 130 employees and annual turnover of £13–14 million, with offices around the world. But it wasn't ready for an exit, and the way the company operated made it vulnerable.

> *In 2000, I hadn't really prepared for exit. Analysys was dependent on me. I managed to sell some big consultancy projects after the collapse, as everybody else was going out of business. But that made me very concerned, because if the company was dependent on me doing the sales, we had a problem.*

In the wake of the dotcom crash, David prepared both the company and the team for a sale.

> *We had these systems in place which enabled everybody to operate things, so I began a programme of three years of devolving stuff and making myself entirely replaceable. So by 2004, I could leave the company with cash in my pocket – which is something that you very rarely do, if ever, with a consultancy company.*

David incentivised his team by giving them some equity, and focused on profitability and increasing turnover to make the company an attractive purchase. He knew that if the company was 'set fair', as he describes it, he would be able to step away and the ship would sail on without him after the acquisition.

> *It was basically the core strategy of the company after 2001:"I'm going to set this up for sale."*

David Cleevely, entrepreneur and investor

Keep going until they realise they need you – Ronjon's story

Ronjon Nag founded his second company, Cellmania, in 1999 to take advantage of the nascent market in apps for mobile phones. But it was the very early days of phones being able to access the internet, and the dotcom crash in 2002 put the company under considerable financial constraints, to the point where Nag had to use the funds from the sale of his first company to keep Cellmania going.

Securing a key contract with Sprint set them on the road to recovery, and big contracts from mobile operators helped the company build a cash base. But they had ambitions, and saw that, with the way the market was going, Cellmania was in a prime position.

Around about 2008 we met with BlackBerry. At the time they were called Research in Motion. And we said, "Look, we've spent nine years at this point working on mobile app stores." Apple had just launched their app store in 2007, a year beforehand. So we said "BlackBerry, do you want some help, because we've done everything you can think of: selling videos, selling music, selling apps, subscription billing, PayPal billing, adding it on to the carrier bill, clubs, you know, games clubs. Do you want some help?"

They said, "No, that's okay. We've got 50 people working on it. Thanks for visiting."

Ronjon Nag, entrepreneur and investor

Cellmania was at the heart of rapid changes in the mobile space, but it was still a small company surrounded by giants and there was a risk that they would get crowded out.

People were afraid for us because Apple had just come out with its app store. They thought it would cripple our business, but actually our business went up because all their competitors wanted an app store too. And people suddenly realised what it was. They went, "Oh yeah, we want one, we want one."

Cellmania looked like it was becoming an acquisition target rather than a partner, but, once again, external circumstances threatened.

2008 was the financial crisis, as we all know, so no one was going to buy any companies. 2009, leftovers of the financial crisis, no one was going to buy any companies. Then came 2010, and now there's a window.

Having partnered with other organisations, Nag recognised that, if Cellmania was to be acquired, he would have to adopt a different strategy.

I hired a bank. But I'm thinking, "Why do I need a bank? I know all the wireless people." By this time, I've been in the industry for 10 years. I know everybody in mobile. But I hired a bank, and the reason for hiring a bank is not because I'm stupid. It's because when the CEO calls up a potential acquirer, the conversation automatically goes into, "Okay, how can we partner? How can we licence?"

When a bank calls up, they know exactly what you're calling for. You might get a quick "no", but you don't beat round the bush. Their client knows this company is probably going to get sold. If they want it, then they need to act.

The bank Nag hired had a list of companies that might be interested in acquiring Cellmania, and RIM was one of them. Based on his earlier experience with RIM, Nag wasn't sure it was worth approaching them.

"They've got their own guys. Why would they want to buy us?" And the banker said, "No, no, no. I think we should go and meet them." So, I say, "Fine. We'll go and meet them." So, we met them and then RIM says, "Oh, right, we need to buy you. We need to buy you right now," not because their guys were stupid, but because the market was moving so quickly. Their corporate development team had realised that they hadn't got time to build what they needed to keep up with the competition.

Ronjon Nag, entrepreneur and investor

Although RIM had been working on their app store for two years, Cellmania had been working on the same challenge for ten years. RIM was running to catch up, and Cellmania was just one of the purchases they made in quick succession to compete against Apple and Google with what became known as Blackberry World.

When the end doesn't mean the end – Carlos' story

Carlos Diniz closed his chain of dental clinics when it went bankrupt. A rapid expansion from 12 to 22 clinics proved unsustainable and the company had to fold. But the failure of his business – and his experiences immediately afterwards – fuelled his drive to be an entrepreneur once more.

I started work after the bankruptcy in probably one of the biggest Portuguese companies. I was contracted to be the head of the clinical company. I hated working there. It was the best thing that could have happened to me, as I learnt that I just didn't want to live like that again…I just felt claustrophobic there. Things didn't happen, it was so slow.

Carlos Diniz, entrepreneur

Carlos learned that one failure was not the end of the world, and having to go back into corporate life reminded him of why he had become an entrepreneur in the first place. It didn't take long for him to redirect his life and start up another business.

Looking backwards now, it's funny. It was not funny two years ago. The bankruptcy was like facing the newspapers – your company appears every two weeks, every day in the news. But after a while, things calm down and people start calling you again, asking for advice, you go back to the beginning and you have opportunities again. So now I am advising a lot of companies. I am a mentor at Nova University – one of the best in Portugal – and besides that, I have my small business, too. But I might be preparing for something bigger in the future.

Carlos Diniz, entrepreneur

THREE THINGS ABOUT THE END OF THE ADVENTURE

- Closing down is hard because you and your team will be emotionally involved, but sometimes it's the right decision if the company isn't making progress.
- Founders should reflect on whether their role is the best for the business. Some founders serve their company better by stepping into a CTO or other role, rather than staying as CEO when the company needs new skills and experience for its next phase.
- Any kind of exit means you are free to start all over again.

Interviewees and contributors

Simon Albury is managing director of Controllis, a power systems hardware and software company. He has 30 years' experience in the telecoms industry.

Jelena Aleksic is a healthcare entrepreneur. She co-founded GeneAdviser (now owned by the NHS) and is director of life sciences consultancy SparkBio Ltd.

Brian Allen is CEO at Rovco, an innovative subsea technology business based in Bristol, UK.

Inger Anson is a corporate lawyer and head of the Cambridge Office of Harrison Clark Rickerbys Ltd. She specialises in helping start-ups navigate their legal requirements.

Max Bautin is managing partner and co-founder of IQ Capital, a seed and early stage tech VC fund that focuses on deep-tech entrepreneurs.

Pilgrim Beart is a serial entrepreneur in the tech space. His latest start-up is DevicePilot, and his previous company, AlertMe, was acquired by British Gas.

Catherine Beech is an entrepreneur and independent biotechnology consultant. She has advised a number of biotech start-ups and is currently director at Better2Know and Locate Therapeutics. She was previously a member of the governing board of the UK Government's Technology Strategy Board (now Innovate UK). She is CEO of Exonate, a drug discovery start-up.

Belinda Bell is a social entrepreneur. She is programme director at Cambridge Social Ventures, a non-executive director of Foundation East and Noise Solution, and a trustee of Mermaids UK.

Ofri Ben-Porat is co-founder and CEO of data company Edgify (formerly known as Pixoneye).

Lord Bilimoria of Chelsea is co-founder of Cobra beer and chairman of Molson Coors Cobra India. Amongst many major leadership roles in India and the UK, he is currently chancellor of the University of Birmingham, chairman of the UK India Business Council, and chairman of the Advisory Board of the Cambridge Judge Business School.

Jon Bradford is founding partner of Motive Partners, an investment firm that focuses on the fintech sector. He is also co-founder of F6S, a network that connects founders and funders.

Tom Britton is co-founder at SyndicateRoom and a non-executive director of the UK Business Angel Association.

David Buxton is CEO and co-founder at Arachnys, a fintech risk detection and regulatory compliance company.

Simon Calver is a partner at investment group BGF Ventures, and chair of the UK Business Angels Association, among others. He was previously CEO of Mothercare and, before that, LoveFilm.

Victor Christou is currently a special advisor at Cambridge Innovation Capital plc., and founder/CEO of Venergise. Previously, he founded two other tech companies, Arborescent and Opsys.

Adam Cleevely is CEO at FutureYou (formerly Cambridge Nutraceuticals), a science-backed online food supplement company. He is also non-executive director at London restaurant Bocca di Lupo.

David Cleevely is chairman of the Raspberry Pi Foundation and Raspberry Pi (Trading) Ltd. He is co-founder of web-based antibody company Abcam, and previously founded telecoms consultancy Analysys.

Sam Cockerill is CEO at Libertine FPE, a company developing novel linear power systems. He is a chartered mechanical engineer and an INSEAD MBA graduate. He is also non-executive director of agricultural supply chain management company Providence Holdings.

Bridget Connell is a start-up investor with Angel Academe and an executive coach and founder at ThinkingPartnerships, after spending over 25 years in senior executive roles.

Dan Cowell is CEO at Psyomics, an early stage biotechnology company working in mental health. He is also non-executive director at techspert.io and Sentinel Oncology.

Tomi Davies is a systems analyst turned tech strategy advisor. He is collaborator-in-chief at Technovision, co-founder of the Lagos Angel Network, and president of the African Business Angel Network.

Shirin Dehghan is a non-executive director at Skimlinks, operating partner at VC fund Frog Capital, and chairwoman of OpenSignal.

Jean de la Verpilliere is CEO and co-founder of Echion Technologies, a company developing next-generation battery technologies for electric vehicles.

Gonçalo de Vasconcelos is founder and CEO of Rnwl, an insuretech company launching in 2020, and co-founder of fintech company SyndicateRoom. He is also a guest lecturer in entrepreneurship and fintech at the University of Cambridge, and a regular contributor to *Forbes*.

Jessica Dick is co-founder of consultancy Five Years Time, which focuses on helping early-stage entrepreneurs navigate the fundraising process. She is also an investment manager at Synergy Growth, and works as a mentor with organisations such as Google Launchpad and Angel Academe.

Carlos Diniz was CEO and co-founder of Portuguese dental chain O Meu Dentista. Currently, he is a board advisor for several tech companies and a business mentor at the Nova School of Business and Economics in Lisbon.

Christopher Dobbing is founder and CEO at the Cambridge Mask Company, developing anti-pollution face masks for the public that incorporate military-grade filtration technology.

Anne Dobrée is head of Cambridge Enterprise Seed Funds, which commercialises technology from the University of Cambridge, and enterprise fellow at the Cambridge Judge Business School. She is also director of Morphogen-IX Limited, and director/ chairman of Psyomics.

Neil D'Souza-Mathew is CTO at Spotta, CTO at smart pest systems company omma.tech, and co-founder at tech consultancy SolidSpark.

Stuart Easton is CEO at Transparent Choice, a company specialising in project prioritization and portfolio management tools.

Zeev Fisher is an IP lawyer and founder of Pekama. He is a registered solicitor (England and Wales) and a registered trademark attorney, having originally passed the Israel Bar Association.

Paul Forster is a tech and early-stage investor after co-founding and heading world-leading multinational job site Indeed up to its acquisition in 2012.

Martin Frost is a serial entrepreneur and investor, currently CEO and co-founder of CMR Surgical, and a director and trustee of Peek Vision.

David Gammon founded family investment office Rockspring after 17 years in investment banking. Rockspring focuses on providing strategic advice and investment to disruptive technology companies.

Andrew Gaule started the Henley Incubator in 2000 and went on to champion open innovation to large corporates. He has founded and led several companies, and is an early-stage investor in tech start-ups.

Elin Haf Davies is founder and CEO of digital health company Aparito, working to improve research and drug development. Among other extreme adventures, she has rowed unsupported across the Atlantic and Indian oceans.

Luke Hakes is a partner at VC investor Octopus Ventures, and is also chair of UMI3 (the University of Manchester's technology transfer office). He began his career as a scientist.

Hermann Hauser is co-founder and director at venture capital firm Amadeus Capital Partners, and has been a serial entrepreneur and investor since founding Acorn Computers in the late 1970s.

Dominic Hill is a jewellery professional and software architect. He is CEO of Atelier Technology, which provides standardised and interactive software for supply chains in the luxury industry.

Nathan Hill is a technology investor and entrepreneur, founder of Qi3 Ventures, and founder and executive chairman of Honest Grapes. He is also an advisory board member for Seraphim Capital's Space Fund, the first early-stage VC fund dedicated to investments in the space sector.

David Holden-White is managing director at techspert.io, an AI company developing better knowledge exchange.

Adam Kerr is founder of Tripism, a platform for business travellers and their employers.

Priya Lakhani is founder CEO of Century Tech, which focuses on AI, machine learning, and blockchain in education, learning and development. She previously founded ethnic sauce brand Masala Masala and, among other awards, was made OBE in 2014.

Greg Law is co-founder and CTO at Undo Ltd, a company developing technology that improves software reliability by finding and resolving defects.

Ramona Liberoff is senior advisor for the SPRING Accelerator, and on the advisory board of ANDigital. She is also COO of the Innogy Innovation Hub in Berlin.

Raymond Luk is founder and CEO of Hockeystick.co in Toronto, founder and CEO of Flow Ventures, and founder of Flow Consulting Inc. He is also a board member of the Toronto Summer Music Foundation, and advisor on the Fintech Advisory Committee of the Ontario Securities Commission.

Emily Mackay is Head of AI and Data Strategy at Congenica, developer of a clinical decision-support platform for analysing complex genomic data.

Chris Mairs is venture partner at Entrepreneur First, an international talent investor that supports individuals and helps them to find co-founders and build technology companies.

William Makant is CEO and co-founder at residential fire-suppression innovator Plumis Ltd.

Neil McArthur set up the business that became TalkTalk and is currently group innovation director at TalkTalk Technology. He is also chairman of the Hamilton Davies Trust, and promotes the entrepreneurial ecosystem of Manchester.

Gemma Milne is a freelance science and tech writer, co-founder and co-host of podcast Science:Disrupt, expert advisor for the

European Commission and Innovate UK, and a venture scout for Backed VC, among other things.

Jonathan Milner co-founded Abcam and is currently deputy chairman of the company. He is an angel investor and non-executive director of several companies, and co-founded the Milner Therapeutics Institute at the University of Cambridge and the Milner Institute for Evolution at the University of Bath.

Chris Mitchell is CEO and founder at Audio Analytic, a company that uses its patented intelligent sound recognition software to enable technology to better understand context through sound.

Yusuf Muhammad is co-founder and design director at residential fire-suppression innovator Plumis.

Ronjon Nag is an entrepreneur and investor. He is currently director of MIT Alumni Angels of Northern California, executive director of GTCardio, founder of Brightswitch, advisor to UC Berkeley Skydeck Accelerator, and a teaching fellow at Stanford University.

Fiona Nielsen is founder and CEO of Repositive, which focuses on ways of working with data in genomics research. She is also CEO of DNAdigest, working on best practices for sharing genomics research data.

Toby Norman is a co-founder and CEO of Simprints, working to apply technology to global health challenges, with support from major NGOs and international companies.

Ronan Perceval is founder and CEO of Phorest Salon Software, which specialises in software for owner-operators in the beauty industry.

Andy Phillipps is an entrepreneur, early-stage tech investor, and a fellow of the Distinguished Career Institute at Stanford University. He co-founded ActiveHotels, which subsequently merged with bookings.org to form what is now booking.com, and is also former chairman of Toptable (now part of Priceline) and a former director of Trainline.

Modwenna Rees-Mogg is executive chairman at The Pluralists Club, co-founder and CEO of AngelNews, and co-founder of CrowdRating. She is also non-executive director of a quoted venture capital trust, and founder CEO of Pitching4Management, among other things.

Dan Reynolds is director at Lungfish Dive Systems, a company developing revolutionary rebreathers for divers.

Suse Reynolds is an angel investor in New Zealand. She sits on the board of the Wellington region's angel network, Angel HQ, and is executive director of the New Zealand Angel Association.

Duncan Robertson is CEO of Dogtooth Technologies, pioneering the use of mass-produced intelligent robots in applications where human labour is hard to recruit.

Alex Schey is Chief Commercial Officer, Electrification at Allison Transmission, and CEO and co-founder of Vantage Power. He was previously founder and president of Racing Green Endurance, a sponsored project that was successful in converting and driving an electric vehicle 26,000km down the Pan-American Highway, the longest road in the world, and continues to inspire and educate.

Yichen Shi is CEO of Axol Bioscience Ltd, a Cambridge (UK) biotech company focusing on providing cell types and reagents for the life science industry.

Toby Schultz is co-founder and CTO at Vantage Power, a company developing unique hybrid diesel-electric retrofit systems for the bus industry. He was also chief vehicle and energy systems engineer on the Racing Green Endurance project (see Alex Schey, above).

Ros Singleton is a telecoms expert, chair of the UK5G Innovation Network Advisory Board, and managing director of UK

Broadband. She also works closely with the UK Government's Department for Digital, Culture, Media and Sport. She is an active mentor and investor in association with Angel Academe.

Sabesan Sithamparanathan is co-founder and CEO at PervasID, which develops passive RFID solutions.

Chris Smith is managing partner at Playfair Capital, and a board director or observer at several tech companies. He also has a portfolio of angel investments.

Joel Solomon is co-founding partner at Renewal Funds, Canada's largest mission venture capital firm. He is co-author of *The Clean Money Revolution: Reinventing Power, Purpose, and Capitalism*, and is active in a number of advisory roles.

Michal Szczesny is CEO at Artfinder, an online marketplace for affordable art.

Rhodri Thomas is CEO at Spectral Edge, an image-processing start-up using advanced computational imaging technology.

Katy Tuncer is an entrepreneur and leadership coach working with early-stage rapid-growth businesses and individual leaders. Her background includes the British military, McKinsey and the Metropolitan Police.

Nigel Walker is head of innovation lending at Innovate UK, and director of Innovate UK Loans Ltd. His experience includes a decade at General Electric and a decade at Deutsche Bank.

Hakim Yadi is CEO and co-founder at Closed Loop Medicine, a therapeutics company focused on care pathways, outcomes and the provision of dynamic personalised regimes.